Cambridge Elements

Elements in Historical Theory and Practice
edited by
Daniel Woolf
Queen's University, Ontario

A HISTORY OF BIG HISTORY

Ian Hesketh
The University of Queensland

Shaftesbury Road, Cambridge CB2 8EA, United Kingdom

One Liberty Plaza, 20th Floor, New York, NY 10006, USA

477 Williamstown Road, Port Melbourne, VIC 3207, Australia

314–321, 3rd Floor, Plot 3, Splendor Forum, Jasola District Centre, New Delhi – 110025, India

103 Penang Road, #05–06/07, Visioncrest Commercial, Singapore 238467

Cambridge University Press is part of Cambridge University Press & Assessment, a department of the University of Cambridge.

We share the University's mission to contribute to society through the pursuit of education, learning and research at the highest international levels of excellence.

www.cambridge.org
Information on this title: www.cambridge.org/9781009005197

DOI: 10.1017/9781009036399

First published 2023

A catalogue record for this publication is available from the British Library.

ISBN 978-1-009-00519-7 Paperback
ISSN 2634-8616 (online)
ISSN 2634-8608 (print)

A History of Big History

Elements in Historical Theory and Practice

DOI: 10.1017/9781009036399
First published online: June 2023

Ian Hesketh
The University of Queensland

Author for correspondence: Ian Hesketh, i.hesketh@uq.edu.au

Abstract: Big History is a seemingly novel approach that seeks to situate human history within a grand cosmic story of life. It claims to do so by uniting the historical sciences in order to construct a linear and accurate timeline of 'threshold moments' beginning with the Big Bang and ending with the present and future development of humanity itself. As well as examining the theory and practice of Big History, this Element considers Big History alongside previous large-scale attempts to unite human and natural history, and includes comparative discussions of the practices of chronology, universal history, and the evolutionary epic.

Keywords: Big History, consilience, thresholds, universal history, chronology

ISBNs: 9781009005197 (PB), 9781009036399 (OC)
ISSNs: 2634-8616 (online), 2634-8608 (print)

Contents

> There now exists no serious intellectual or scientific or philosophical barriers to a broad unification of historical scholarship.
>
> David Christian, 'A Single Historical Continuum' (2017)

1 Introduction: What Is Big History?

According to its practitioners and proponents, Big History presents a story of life that everyone needs to know. This is because Big History situates human history within a truly grand narrative of life that begins with the Big Bang and ends with the future development of humanity. It is described as a 'modern origin story', but its ostensible novelty lies in its synthesis of the historical sciences of cosmology, geology, biology, and anthropology that provides a scientific framework for understanding the history of the human species within the broadest possible context. The proponents of Big History, many of whom lived through the height of the Cold War and the multiple nuclear crises it engendered, hope that Big History will enable its readers to come to terms with some of the large-scale challenges that now confront the human species. The proliferation of nuclear weapons remains one those challenges, but it has been joined in recent years by the ubiquitous issue of anthropogenic climate change.[1] Humans have become so powerful that their actions now threaten to undermine the conditions that made human flourishing viable in the first place. Big History seeks to provide an overarching context to this predicament and thus the intellectual tools that are required to envision viable solutions to it.

In order to achieve this fundamental goal, practitioners advocate transforming the way history is taught by embracing recent methodological trends of large-scale analysis that eschew traditional historiographical boundaries such as those separating history from prehistory and society from nature. These key aspects of Big History will be briefly discussed in Sections 1.1 to 1.2 along with a description of this Element's argument (Section 1.3).

1.1 Big History and Pedagogy

First and foremost, Big History emerged as a challenge to the growing specialization of the academy, which is especially evident in the discipline of history, typically divided as it is into geographical and temporal areas of specialty. David Christian tells us that he invented Big History in order to challenge that specialization, which was turning students away from subjects like history because the knowledge produced was so fragmented. Students needed to see instead how historical knowledge could be fitted within a big picture. Trained as

[1] On the ethical underpinnings of Big History, see Hughes-Warrington, *Big and Little Histories*, chapter 9.

a historian, Christian decided to teach history from the broadest perspective imaginable and did so by bringing together scholars from across the sciences and the humanities to construct a course that told the scientific story of life. He named the course 'Big History'.[2]

Since Christian began teaching Big History at the end of the 1980s at Macquarie University in Sydney, Australia, it has grown immensely. Christian has subsequently been joined by a group of like-minded scholars from a range of disciplinary backgrounds who set out to provide their own contributions to the Big History narrative. The most notable of these is the Dutch biochemist and cultural anthropologist Fred Spier. He wrote what is likely the first monograph to be published under the 'Big History' label and has focused subsequent work on establishing the scientific basis for Big History.[3] Other leading practitioners include the late American historian of education Cynthia Stokes Brown (1938–2017), who wrote the first history of Big History for general readers after retiring from teaching in 2001, and the Australian historian Craig Benjamin, who specializes in the history of Central Asia and has produced multiple courses in the realm of world history for the Teaching Company's Great courses programme.[4] He also wrote, with Christian and Brown, the first university-level Big History textbook.[5] And Christian himself has written multiple book-length studies of Big History from a specialized monograph to a *New York Times* bestseller.[6] As well as being attracted to the holistic nature of the Big History narrative, what unites these diverse scholars is a desire to change the way history is taught while letting that transformation be a guide for subsequent research and writing. And, in some ways, they have been remarkably successful in achieving their goals.

Big History is now taught at universities around the world and is particularly well established in Australia. It has also grown as a specialized field in its own right with the establishment of the International Big History Association (IBHA) in 2010. The IBHA has subsequently organized several international conferences and, since 2017, began producing the peer-reviewed *Journal of Big History*. The journal typically includes articles that debate some of the finer points of the Big History narrative, such as how the 'metapatterns' of Big History can best be represented, and the relationship between cosmic myths and evolutionary survival.[7] What the journal shows is that even though Big

---

[2] Christian, 'The Case for "Big History"'.

[3] Spier, *The Structure of Big History*; and Spier, *Big History and the Future of Humanity*.

[4] Brown, *Big History*; and Benjamin, *The First Silk Roads Era*. Benjamin's Teaching Company course can be found here: www.thegreatcourses.com/professors/craig-g-benjamin.

[5] Christian, Brown, and Benjamin, *Big History*.

[6] Christian, *Maps of Time*; and Christian, *Origin Story*. See also his most recent *Future Stories*.

[7] Volk, 'The Metapattern of General Evolutionary Dynamics and the Three Dynamical Realms of Big History'; and Lineweaver, 'Cosmic Perspectives and the Myths We Need to Survive'.

History emerged to challenge the growing specialization of history, it has not been immune from producing its own specialized discourse that is reliant on jargon like 'threshold moments', 'Goldilocks circumstances', and 'energy flows'.

At the same time, Big History has also moved beyond the university, in large part thanks to the enduring interest and deep pockets of American billionaire and philanthropist Bill Gates. Gates and Christian founded the Big History Project in 2011, a website devoted to providing pedagogical materials for high schools and individual teachers interested in integrating Big History into their curriculum. Its success spawned the Open Educational Resources (OER) Project, which provides resources for both Big History and world history. As explained on the website, the OER Project is 'a coalition of educators and historians focused on boosting student engagement and achievement through transformational social studies programs'. Its selling point is that it 'offer[s] teachers better curricula and a vibrant community'.[8] As a result of the OER Project and its predecessor, Big History has become entrenched in high-school education, particularly in the United States and Australia.[9]

1.2 Big History and Scientific History

Big History is also part of a larger contemporary trend that seeks to situate human history within larger time frames that are informed by scientific advance. Indeed, the separation of the 'two cultures' that has, since C. P. Snow (1905–80), become an underlying assumption and trope of academic discourse has come under scrutiny in recent years. So too has the rationale for limiting the terrain of history as a discipline to the era of written records. For Harvard professor of history Daniel Lord Smail, for instance, this central limitation is a survival from the discipline's foundation in biblical timescales, where everything before the Christian era was deemed 'prehistory'. Smail advocates crossing what he calls history's temporal Rubicon, arguing that there are important factors that have shaped human history that cannot be understood properly without taking a much deeper view of the past. He refers in particular to adaptations that were formed as humans originally evolved as a species, and that need to be considered in order to understand even the most recent of historical processes and developments. This 'deep history', as Smail and others call it, thus seeks to apply recent theories

[8] www.oerproject.com/FAQ. Some have questioned Gates's motivations and actions in this space: see 'Why the Big History Project Funded by Bill Gates is Alarming'; and Sorkin, 'So Bill Gates Has This Idea for a History Class . . .'.

[9] For case studies on the teaching of the Big History Project, see Sullivan, 'The *Big History Project* in Australia'; and Robert Bain, 'Crossing Thresholds'.

of evolutionary biology and evolutionary psychology in order to provide deeply consequential insights about more recent human history.[10]

Moreover, well before the arrival of deep history, environmental historians had eschewed the supposed divisions between human and natural history and between prehistory and history proper. Alfred Crosby's *The Columbian Exchange* (1972), for instance, is often identified as a groundbreaking book that recognized how the history of expansion and colonization is entangled with the history of disease and domestication, as it carefully analyzed the large-scale biological and cultural consequences that resulted from the so-called discovery of the New World.[11] More recently, environmental historians have taken the lead in historicizing the impact of human development on the Earth itself. Most notable is J. R. McNeill's *Something New Under the Sun* (2000), which explored the way that humans had, in the twentieth century, transformed the Earth's ecosystems to such an extent that the Earth and its various systems are now fundamentally altered. He thus situated his environmental history of the twentieth century within a much longer history of the Earth, providing insight into the transformative nature of recent human development while informing subsequent investigations into the nature of anthropogenic climate change.[12]

A related though ultimately quite different attempt to bring together science and history over the *longue durée* is the 'planetary history' of Dipesh Chakrabarty. For Chakrabarty, the recent acceleration of global climate change that has been brought about by human development has meant that the geological timescale typically associated with tens of thousands of years has now collided with the human timescales represented by the more recent industrial and capital development of modern society. Processes that were once viewed as quite separate, such as the systems that determine the climate of the Earth and those having to do with capital accumulation and modernization, now need to be brought into conversation with one another. There is, unfortunately, no easy way to do this. But Chakrabarty recognizes the need to try, and so he writes history in a new way in order to think about humans whose history and development must be put in relation to other biological and geological actors.[13]

[10] Smail, *On Deep History and the Brain*. This is not to be confused with the 'deep history' produced by followers of Brian Swimme and Thomas Berry, who seek to produce a spiritually deep account of humanity's cosmic and spiritual journey. On this form of deep history, see Kelly, *Becoming Gaia*.

[11] See Hughes-Warrington, *Big and Little Histories*, 144.

[12] On the relationship between McNeill's work and that of Earth System Science, see Thomas, Williams, and Zalasiewicz, *The Anthropocene*, 133.

[13] Chakrabarty, *The Climate of History in a Planetary Age*.

While Big History follows a rationale similar to those of deep history, environmental history, and planetary history, in the sense that its practitioners recognize that human history needs to be understood within the framework of biological and geological timescales and theories, what sets it apart is its desire for universality. This universality is what lies at the basis of the entire Big History endeavour, and is symbolized by Christian's suggestion that it provides an origin story that is both about everyone and for everyone. In this regard it shares a great deal with popular studies of the history of humans *as a species*, a genre typified by the work of the geographer Jared Diamond.[14] Diamond's *The Rise and Fall of the Third Chimpanzee* (1991), for instance, explored what made humans different from closely related species of primates in order to convince readers about humanity's special capabilities to overcome the existential threats posed by nuclear weapons and climate change. Diamond's work inspired the medieval historian Yuval Noah Harari to write the astonishingly successful *Sapiens* (2011), which told the story of how humans came to dominate other species from their African origins up to the present. This is a story Harari continued into the future with *Homo Deus* (2015), a book that imagined a future scenario where the very algorithms created by intelligent humans ultimately lead to their downfall. What these works all share is the desire to synthesize the facts and theories discerned from multiple scientific disciplines while transcending geological, biological, and human timescales in order to tell a singular story about the nature and history of the human species.

This desire is also what is central to Big History, namely to produce a single and universal narrative of history that will include the most important facts relevant to humanity's history. These facts are then to be ordered along the lines discerned from contemporary science, not as a series of disconnected theories and laws, but rather as integrated paradigms of knowledge that are brought together by the second law of thermodynamics and universal evolution. That the sciences can be integrated in this way is a claim that the proponents of Big History largely seek to justify by an appeal to E. O. Wilson's (1929–2021) notion of 'consilience', which suggests that there is an underlying universal reality that connects the various sciences that can be represented by synthetic laws of nature.[15] It is the task of Big History to use these few unifying laws to form the basis of the Big History narrative.

If the science of Big History is universalizing, it follows that so is the narrative derived from it. That narrative, moreover, is referred to as a 'modern

[14] It should be noted that this genre is itself clearly derived from works of ethology from the 1960s that explained the emergence of humans as the result of a 'killer instinct'. See Milam, *Creatures of Cain*; and Weidman, *Killer Instinct*.

[15] Wilson, *Consilience*.

origin story' or a 'modern secular myth'. While the idea of a 'modern origin story' may seem like a contradiction, big historians stress that the modernizing dimension of science is not in conflict with the mythopoeic nature of the narrative that is produced. This is because, as Christian notes in *Origin Story*, attempting to tell the story of where humans came from and how they developed over time is a universal social need. Christian argues, therefore, that Big History just happens to be the most recent attempt to do what all human societies have sought to do, namely situate their lives within grand cosmic stories of life.[16] The difference between the story of Big History and that of previous origin stories is that because Big History is based on modern science, it is well and truly about everybody. But just how different is Big History from previous forms of large-scale history,[17] and does it overcome the quite narrow and Eurocentric nature of its predecessors?

1.3 Big History in Historical Context

This Element seeks to articulate and examine Big History's theory and practice from within a historical context. A central focus of this examination concerns the claim that Christian and other proponents of Big History make, namely, that because the story is centrally about the human species, the narrative is necessarily about and for everyone. On one hand, this universalizing claim fails to appreciate just how much the Big History narrative conflicts with many of the very origin stories that it seeks to displace. And, on the other, the modern origin story of Big History is one that is specific to a particular tradition of Christian cosmic history, a universalizing tradition that seeks to tell the whole story of life from a rather narrow perspective. Moreover, Big History's generic claims of being based on modern science mask its roots in contentious philosophical theories about the unity of science and the complementarity of disparate temporalities.

With these matters in mind, Section 2 of this Element seeks to tell a history of Big History, that is explore some of Big History's predecessors in order to draw out some important themes that connect Big History to a particular tradition of large-scale history writing. The point will be to show that the very structure of the Big History narrative, such as its linear progressivism that is divided into a series of thresholds, is indebted to the providentialism of Christian universal histories that envisioned the unfolding of history as a series of 'days' or 'epochs' leading to the eschaton. While the secularization

[16] Christian, *Origin Story*, 6–9.

[17] For Big History as 'largest-scale' history as distinguished from forms of 'mere' 'large-scale' history, see Megill, '"Big History" Old and New'.

of universal history with the Enlightenment of the eighteenth century, and the rise of positivism and the science of evolution in the nineteenth and twentieth centuries, extended the timeframe of the past, the overarching form of the story largely remained the same.

Section 3 of this Element then turns to a critical examination of the more recent emergence of Big History, focusing in particular on the points of connection to previous forms of large-scale history, but also on those that supposedly set it apart. Like these other forms of large-scale history, it is deterministic, and yet it purports to ascribe agency to its readers in their act of becoming conscious of the story of life imparted in its pages. This Element argues that Big History relies on the same sense of history that motivated the earlier histories, and similarly utilizes the same mythopoeic scientistic rhetoric to justify its truth claims. It is a narrative, moreover, that privileges necessity at the expense of contingency, often to the detriment of its chief message.

2 A History of Big History

When David Christian originally made his 'Case for Big History' in a 1991 article in the *Journal of World History*, he stressed the novelty of his newly developed approach, which originated in the classroom.[18] Christian explained that he had grown frustrated with the increasing specialization of history research and teaching, and believed that it was contributing to a sense of fragmentation and division among his students and humanity at large. While his early work was quite specialized, and focused on the drinking habits of nineteenth-century Russian peasants, he later considered broader connections across space and time informed by the burgeoning fields of environmental and world history. A result of this research was what Christian called a 'trans-ecological study' that considered the multiple exchanges between pastoralist and agrarian societies that occurred along the Silk Roads, a study that further contributed to the integration of Afro-Eurasian history.[19] It was in part a recognition of the pedagogical value of such large, interdisciplinary studies that led him to think about new ways of teaching history from similarly holistic perspectives. He thus began teaching an interdisciplinary course that included lectures from professors in the sciences and the humanities, a course that told the story of humanity, but situated within the grandest historical context possible, one that began with the Big Bang.

[18] Christian, 'The Case for "Big History"'.

[19] Christian, *Living Water*; and Christian, 'Silk Roads or Steppe Roads?'

Christian explained that once he realised that he did not have to adhere to history's traditional disciplinary boundaries represented by the era of written records, it became necessary for him to continue to expand the scale backwards in time until reaching the very beginning.

> We cannot fully understand the past few millennia without understanding the far longer period of time in which all members of our species lived as gatherers and hunters, and without understanding the changes that led to the emergence of the earliest agrarian communities and the first urban civilizations. Paleolithic society, in its turn, cannot be fully understood without some idea of the evolution of our own species over several million years. That however requires some grasp of the history of life on earth, and so on. Such arguments may seem to lead us to an endless regress, but it is clear that they do not. According to modern Big Bang cosmology, the universe itself has a history, with a clear and identifiable beginning somewhere between 10 and 20 billion years ago. We can say nothing of what happened before this time; indeed time itself was created in the Big Bang. So this time scale is different from others. If there is an absolute framework for the study of the past, this is it. If the past can be studied whole, this is the scale within which to do it.

From the very beginning, then, Christian envisioned Big History as the study of the past as a 'whole'. And, in order to study the past from such a holistic perspective, Christian argued that the historian needed to go back to the Big Bang, which provided the 'absolute framework for the study of the past'.[20] About a decade later, Christian published a monograph, *Maps of Time*, which provided a clear example of what such a history would look like, as it began with an analysis of the energy unleashed by the Big Bang, which set the stage for the progressive complexity of life to follow, culminating in the origin and development of the human species. But was this approach genuinely new?

In subsequent publications, Christian acknowledged that he was not the first to attempt to produce such a large-scale historical narrative. In an essay in *History and Theory*, Christian argued that Big History owed its origins to a form of historical writing that pre-dated the professionalization of history. Christian explained that as history became more formalized in the nineteenth century, along the empirical and inductive lines articulated by Leopold von Ranke (1795–1886) and others, speculative and large-scale histories were 'expelled' from the profession for not living up to the new archival demands of the document-based historian. Big History, therefore, represented a return to this pre-disciplinary formation when the historian was not so constrained by the

[20] Christian, 'The Case for "Big History"', 224–5.

documentary evidence and could produce histories that stretched across time and space. This long-forgotten form of history, Christian claimed, was known as 'universal history'.[21]

For Christian, what connected universal history and Big History was the fact that both were attempts to construct large-scale historical narratives that sought to explain and relate the most important human and natural events while linking the present with the past. He recognized, however, that earlier universal histories tended to be narrowly conceived despite their claims to universality, based on the 'limited information' that was available at the time that projected 'onto a nearly empty historiographical canvas a sort of shadow identity of Europe'.[22] As well as being Eurocentric, such histories also often relied on poorly understood scientific processes and timescales. It was precisely with regard to these problematic areas that Big History represented an upgrade. As Christian explained, by shifting the focus to include the human species in general rather than specific classes, races, or nations, Big History was able to transcend the narrow racialized perspectives that had corrupted previous universal histories. And, thanks to advances in radiocarbon, genetic, and cosmic dating techniques, Big History was also able to date accurately astronomical, geological, and biological events in a way that was unimaginable before the mid-twentieth century.[23] A clear symbol of how Big History utilizes this scientific accuracy to inform its narrative is in the construction of a timeline that emplots Big History's key events.[24]

As the timeline makes clear, the Big History narrative is structured by a series of 'thresholds'. While these thresholds are assigned relatively specific dates, given the vast timescales that are involved their accuracy is much less precise than might be expected. And, as we will see in later sections (Sections 3.2–3.3), the precise nature of these thresholds is speculative. What is worth exploring further at this point, however, is the fact that the Big History story was emplotted as a series of thresholds or stages in the first place, stages that were meant to integrate the human past with the events of the natural world, a practice that had been central to universal history, as well as to other large-scale narratives of the Christian tradition. The following sections (Sections 2.1–2.4) seek to explore more fully these earlier forms of Big History.

---

[21] Christian, 'The Return of Universal History', 6–27, 12 ('expelled').

[22] Christian, 'The Return of Universal History', 17.

[23] Christian, 'The Return of Universal History', 17–19.

[24] The timeline can be found here: https://blogdotbighistoryprojectdotcom.files.wordpress.com/2016/01/lbh2.jpg (accessed 3 June 2022).

2.1 Sacred Universal Histories and Theories of the Earth

For big historians, what makes Big History different from other origin stories is that, in the words of Christian, 'it builds on the global traditions of modern science', and therefore 'lacks a creator god'.[25] What such claims about Big History's reliance on the traditions of global science fail to acknowledge is how the very structure of the Big History narrative is embedded in a sense of history that originated in a quite specific origin story articulated in the book of Genesis. This foundational text in the Judeo-Christian tradition presents a linear view of history, with a moment of Creation when history began with the creation of the universe, followed by a series of events from the creation of plants, animals, and then humans (Adam and Eve) to an extinction event (Flood) that set the stage for humanity to repopulate, and to migrate throughout, the Earth. This story combined events of both natural and human history that, taken together, explained the origin, development, and destiny of life all focused on the central figure of 'man'. This story, along with the other historical books of the Old Testament, provided the evidentiary basis for a tradition of history writing that lasted a millennium, namely, the tradition of universal history, which has links to related forms of history such as the practice of chronology.

It is important to note that there were other forms of universal history that pre-date the Christian version, such as universal Chinese and Greek histories. Sima Qian's (*c.*145–*c.*86 BC) formative *Shiji* (*c.*100 BC), for instance, covered 2,500 years of Chinese dynastic history, divided into five sections (Annals, Tables, Treatises, Hereditary Houses, and Biographies), with each section relying on a different style of analysis.[26] This vast and diverse history of China became, in the words of G. E. R. Lloyd, 'the chief model used by all subsequent Chinese historiography'.[27] A tradition of universal history was also established in ancient Greece, as historiographers such as Ephorus (*c.*405–*c.*330 BC) and Diodorus (*fl.* first century BC) wrote large-scale histories that situated the Greek past within the context of the expanding known world.[28] While these earlier forms of universal history were similar to the Christian version in that they sought to present fairly comprehensive views of the past, they relied on quite different conceptions of historical development, with the Chinese presenting a multiplicity of narratives and overlapping timelines and the Greek an ultimately cyclical story of eternal recurrence.

In contrast, central to Christian universal history was the attempt to reconcile the recent past of expansion and conflict, referred to as profane history, with the large-scale narrative of the deep past that was presented in the authoritative

[25] Christian, *Origin Story*, 9.
[26] See Nienhauser, 'Sima Qian and the *Shiji*'.
[27] Lloyd, 'Epilogue', 614.
[28] See Marincola, 'Universal History from Ephorus to Diodorus'.

sacred texts of the Bible. An early, formative example of universal history is the *City of God* by St Augustine of Hippo (354–430). Augustine's purpose was to challenge the Greek notion of eternal recurrence in order to establish the doctrine of salvation, something that is only possible if there is an absolute beginning and an eventual end point, the proof of which was provided by the authority of the Scriptures, as opposed to the events of profane history. This linear and teleological notion of history, which envisioned the past beginning in an ultimate origin and progressing towards a predestined end, formed the foundation for the Christian approach to universal history, and, subsequently, to the Islamic version of universal history as well.[29]

That teleological narrative of Christian universal history was typically organized by reference to a series of epochs or ages that reflected key biblical events. This was a genre convention established by Augustine, who divided his historical narrative into seven 'ages', which corresponded to the central historical events of the Bible: (1) Adam; (2) Deluge; (3) Abraham; (4) David; (5) Babylonian Captivity; (6) Birth of Christ; and (7) the Millennium.[30] The central thread running throughout was that this history gave evidence of a tension or struggle between the earthly and heavenly states, between the Devil and God. The purpose of universal histories like that of Augustine's was not just to put more recent events within a sacred historical framework but more so to insist on how Providence had guided the overall shape of the past in order to anticipate the end times.[31]

This linear, sacred form of history was accorded a sense of temporal precision in the Renaissance due to the contributions of 'chronology', a discipline constructed by theologians, natural philosophers, and historians. The chief task of chronologists was to synchronize Jewish and Roman history along a single linear timescale that would enable a clear understanding of the precise relations of past events to one another as well as to the present and future. The Bible was the central but not the only historical source that was utilized in dating precisely when the most important events occurred in the past. Other sources brought to bear on the analysis included calendrical and astronomical data as well as philological and historical studies of Near Eastern history. One of the innovations of this practice was the establishment of the 'Julian Period' by Joseph Justus Scaliger (1540–1609), an arbitrary timeline that triangulated astronomical and calendrical cycles to determine the precise dates of sacred events.[32] A singular calendrical system was also created, *Anno Mundi*

[29] Marsham, 'Universal Histories in Christendom and the Islamic World *c.*700–*c.*1400', 437. Note that an analysis of Islamic universal history is beyond the scope of this Element.

[30] Ghosh, 'Some Theories of Universal History', 4.

[31] See, for instance, Löwith, *Meaning in History*, chapter 9.

[32] On Scaliger and the Julian Period, see Grafton, 'Joseph Scaliger and Historical Chronology'; and Rudwick, *Earth's Deep History*, 14–15.

(AM), that enabled the plotting of events based on their relation to Creation. For many chronologists, the underlying rationale for engaging in this process was to map out the exact length of time that separated the present from Creation in view of predicting the eschaton. This was the main reason why discerning precisely when God had created all things became a particularly contentious preoccupation for chronologists.

One of the most best-known chronologists was the Anglican Bishop James Ussher (1581–1656), whose *Annals of the Old Covenant* (1650–4) claimed that God created the universe precisely at twilight on 23 October 4004 BC. Like other chronologists, Ussher relied on evidence provided by the stories of the Bible to infer the exact date for Creation, one that was made by adding up the generations referred to in Genesis up to the Flood (Genesis 5:1–7:6).[33] This involved relatively simple arithmetic but also certain assumptions such as whether or not Adam's 130th birthday should fall on 130 or 131 AM. Such seemingly inconsequential decisions could lead to a wide range of possible dates.[34] Isaac Newton (1643–1727) and Scaliger are just two of the most prominent chronologists who offered alternative dates for Creation based on competing chronological models.[35] Ussher's particular chronology became more popular, however, and came to symbolize the young Earth perspective of the early modern period that was often ridiculed in the nineteenth century and beyond, because it was discreetly printed in the margins of the King James Bible.[36]

The date of Creation was just the most conspicuous of the key dates that chronologists sought to establish. Chronologists also sought to plot out the dates for all the key epochs in the Bible. For his part, Ussher sought to establish the main events that represented the seven ages of world history that appeared in Augustine's *City of God*. Like most other chronologists, Ussher's analysis of these events included the prediction of a future, eighth event: the end of the world following the second coming of Jesus.

While the dating of Creation relied entirely on biblical sources, this was not the case with the dating of subsequent events, particularly the Flood, for which chronologists relied on a mixture of evidence provided by Scripture and by natural history. It was recognized that, as a global geological event, the Flood would have left evidence in the very structure of the Earth, which led to a particular kind of chronological commentary that sought to reconcile the evidence provided by Scripture on one hand with that provided by nature on

[33] Poole, *The World Makers*, 39–40. [34] Poole, *The World Makers*, 41.

[35] On Newton's chronological practices and their connection to his related studies of the prophecies in Scripture, see Schilt, *Isaac Newton and the Study of Chronology*. For Scaliger, see Grafton, 'Joseph Scaliger and Historical Chronology'; and Grafton, 'Scaliger's Chronology'.

[36] Woolf, *A Global History of History*, 193; and Rudwick, *Earth's Deep History*, 29.

the other. As Martin Rudwick explains, this was the foundation for a sense of history that buttressed subsequent attempts to plot out human and natural history along a linear timeline:

> This strong sense of history gave the Judeo-Christian tradition an underlying structure that is closely analogous to the modern view of the Earth's deep history (and cosmic history) as similarly *finite and directional*. More specifically, the science of scholarly chronology, as a way of plotting human history with quantitative accuracy and of dividing it into a qualitatively significant sequence of eras and periods, was closely analogous to the modern science of '*geochronology*', which tries to give a similar kind of precision and structure to the Earth's deep history, dividing it in the same way into eras and periods.[37]

While it is true that the 6,000-year timeline provided by the science of chronology is a tiny sliver compared to the 13.8-billion-year timeline of Big History, structurally they are similar because they are informed by the same sense of history, one that is directional, finite, and divided by a series of ages or epochs.

A prominent example of an early modern universal history that incorporated the findings of chronology was Jacques-Bénigne Bossuet's *Discourse on Universal History* (1681). Bossuet was a preacher in the court of Louis XIV, and tutor to Louis's heir, and he was preoccupied with ensuring that Louis and his son conformed to their roles as Christian princes. This was all the more important because Bossuet believed that humankind was living through a truly historic moment that could only be properly appreciated within the context of a universal history. He therefore wrote the *Discourse* to instruct Louis XIV and his heir (it was dedicated to 'Le Dauphin') to learn to distinguish between the various past ages as well as to understand the unity that connects all of history. 'Even if history were useless to other men,' Bossuet explained in the first sentence, 'princes should be made to read it.'[38]

To ease the Dauphin's understanding of universal history, Bossuet divided his study into three parts: the first gave an outline of the epochs and ages of history; the second then explored the religious meanings of those epochs, stressing the continuity of the Church; and the third focused on the rise and fall of empires in relation to Providence. It was important to provide the Prince with such a broad perspective so that he would be able to 'perceive, as in one glance, the entire sequence of time'. It was in this way that Bossuet likened his universal history to a map of all maps.

> This kind of universal history is to the history of every country and of every people what a world map is to particular maps. In a particular map you see all the details of a kingdom or a province as such. But a general map teaches you

[37] Rudwick, *Earth's Deep History*, 29. [38] Bossuet, *Discourse on Universal History*, 3.

> to place these parts of the world in their context; you see what Paris or the Ile-de-France is in the kingdom, what the kingdom is in Europe, and what Europe is in the world.[39]

It was a 'map of time', as David Christian might put it.

The first part of Bossuet's universal history mostly re-examined territory already mapped out by Augustine and other universal histories, as Bossuet appropriated the seven-ages structure of *City of God,* although he supplemented those ages with a number of smaller epochs. He also added more temporal specificity, appropriated from chronologists. For the 'First Epoch: Adam, or the Creation', Bossuet stated that it 'begins with a grand spectacle: God creating heaven and earth through his word and making man in his image (1 A.M., 4004 BC)', thereby reproducing the date of Creation proposed by Ussher. He stressed to his princely reader that this was a story originally told by Moses, 'the first historian, the most sublime philosopher, and the wisest of legislators[.] On this foundation he builds his history as well as his teaching and his laws.'[40]

Bossuet juxtaposed the events of sacred history with those of profane history, mainly by describing conflicts and the rise and fall of empires. The only empire that truly mattered, however, was 'the empire of the Son of Man [Jesus]: and this empire is to stand when all the others fall, since it alone is promised eternal duration'.[41] The ultimate message that Bossuet sought to impart with his universal history was that history has a clear design and direction that can be discerned only when viewed as a whole. He recognized that when events are considered in isolation they will appear as coincidental, or perhaps due to fortune. Such views, however, are a product of ignorance of the higher, eternal foresight that is made apparent from the perspective of universal history. 'What is coincidence to our uncertain foresight is concerted design to a higher foresight, that is, to the eternal foresight which encompasses all causes and all effects in a single plan,' Bossuet explained. 'Thus all things concur to the same end; and it is only because we fail to understand the whole design that we see coincidence or strangeness in particular events.'[42]

While universal histories like Bossuet's were typically most concerned with aligning the political events of the human past with a grander sense of history informed by its providential design, a related genre sought to situate sacred history within contemporary philosophical and scientific theories of the Earth and its development. The English theologian and natural philosopher Thomas Burnet (1635–1715), for instance, sought to reconcile Cartesian physics with

---

[39] Bossuet, *Discourse on Universal History*, 4.
[40] Bossuet, *Discourse on Universal History*, 9.
[41] Bossuet, *Discourse on Universal History*, 301.
[42] Bossuet, *Discourse on Universal History*, 374.

a biblical understanding of history by creating an overarching theory of life that linked up the history of humanity with the history of the Earth. Burnet appropriated from Descartes the idea that the Earth is a series of layers that surround a core of hot molten lava. But Descartes's theory was problematic for Burnet, and for other orthodox Christians like him, because its developmentalism was not embedded in a Christian timeframe. For Descartes, the Earth's history was analogous to the history of other planets; it was therefore irrelevant how the Earth's history may have related to the events of sacred history. For his part, Burnet added the missing sacred dimension to Descartes's system by situating it within a progressive, developmental framing that was thoroughly integrated with the historical events of the Bible.[43]

Burnet's *Sacred Theory of the Earth* (1680–9) thus opened with a defence of a literal interpretation of certain biblical events that Burnet claimed could be established via an appropriate understanding of Cartesian physics in application to the Earth's development. As was nicely illustrated by the *Sacred Theory*'s frontispiece in the 1684 English translation, Burnet argued that the Earth had gone through a series of stages of development, notably the Creation and the Flood, and would eventually go through a final stage that would bring about the future Conflagration.[44] Burnet's rationale for establishing this large-scale history of the Earth was in order to promote, in the words of William Poole, 'a model of God's general providence ("laws of nature") that would limit the need for the philosopher to appeal to special providence ("miracles")'.[45] Under Burnet's scheme, natural and human history could be understood entirely by reference to natural laws that were established by the science of physics.

Burnet was not the only writer in the late seventeenth century to construct such grand theories of the Earth. A competing version was produced by the theologian and mathematician William Whiston (1667–1752) in his book, *A New Theory of the Earth* (1696). Whiston's 'new theory' was structurally similar to Burnet's, with the important exception that instead of relying on Cartesian physics, Whiston utilized the physical theories of fellow Englishman, Isaac Newton. *A New Theory of the Earth* relies so extensively and explicitly on Newtonian physics that Stephen Snobelen considers it the 'first full-length popularization of the natural philosophy of [Newton's] *Principia*'.[46] For our purposes, what is important about Whiston's appropriation of the *Principia* (1687), is that Whiston argued that it was not a terrestrial process that caused the

43 Poole, *The World Makers*, 57–8.

44 For Burnet's frontispiece, see www.britishmuseum.org/collection/object/P_1850-0223-497 (accessed 3 June 2022).

45 Poole, *The World Makers*, 59.

46 Snobelen, 'William Whiston, Isaac Newton and the Crisis of Publicity', 573.

Flood but a cosmic one, specifically a comet. Newton believed that comets were providential agents that had brought about substantial change in the cosmos, a view that Whiston embraced in his suggestion that 'the vapours of a comet tail might be sufficient to bring about the torrential rains of the Noachic Flood'.[47] It followed that it would be a comet that would cause the Conflagration as well.[48] With Whiston, the physics of the universe was brought into harmony with the history of the Earth, along with the biblical narrative of that history.

In the early modern period, therefore, we find a range of related genres of large-scale history that sought to integrate natural and human history in linear and teleological narratives. That they relied on the Bible as an authoritative source should not dissuade us from appreciating the sense and structure of history that reinforced these narratives: a holistic understanding of the past, with a clear beginning and end, structured by a series of clearly defined and datable periods of time. As we will see, the secularization of universal history would do little to alter this overarching structure of history; what changes is that the biblical authority that was appropriated in order to produce such narratives was displaced in favour of impersonal laws of nature, a process already underway in sacred theories of the Earth produced by the likes of Burnet and Whiston.

2.2 Secular and Positivist Universal Histories

Although sacred universal histories continued to flourish, particularly in the sixteenth and seventeenth centuries, the recognition that there exist vastly different cultures that came about due to the voyages that mariners and would-be conquerors made to lands previously unknown to Europeans problematized the plausibility of supposedly universal histories based on literal readings of the Bible. As early as the seventeenth century, for instance, the French theologian Isaac La Peyrère (1596–1676) posited the existence of what he called 'pre-Adamites', humans that existed before the creation of Adam. While this radical theory sought to establish an earlier, separate moment of Creation for humans than the one that appears in the Genesis account, La Peyrère was ultimately seeking to reconcile Scripture with the existence of peoples who could not be fitted into the literal Adamic narrative.[49] The pre-Adamite hypothesis also enabled the recognition of the possibility of a much deeper and uncertain human past,[50] one that was paralleled by the suggestion by some theologians and scholars that the 'days' of Creation discussed in Genesis actually represented unknown durations of time, thereby extending cosmic and geological

[47] Snobelen, 'William Whiston, Isaac Newton and the Crisis of Publicity', 576.
[48] Rudwick, *Earth's Deep History*, 61.
[49] On the history of La Peyrère's pre-Adamite hypothesis, see Livingstone, *Adam's Ancestors*.
[50] Poole, *The World Makers*, 35.

history as well. These inelegant solutions tended to show the profound difficulties that confronted universal historians who sought to make sense of historical phenomena that did not conform to the biblical narrative. Even some proponents of sacred universal history, such as Jean Bodin (1530–96), recognized that the difficulties of reconciling the theological with the profane were so great that producing a single narrative of history was impossible.[51] The fossil discoveries of subsequent centuries and the related recognition of an ancient Earth would make defending sacred universal history even more difficult.

While sacred universal history declined in the eighteenth century, the ideal of constructing a universal history, though purged of theology, was advocated and attempted by several prominent philosophers and historians. Voltaire's (1694–1778) *Essay on Universal History, the Manners, and Spirit of Nations* (1756), for instance, has often been considered a significant representation of the shift from sacred to secular universal history as the book was written in diametrical opposition to the theistic perspective of Bossuet's *Discourse on Universal History*.[52] Tamara Griggs, however, stresses that the shift from sacred to secular was much less sudden than this implies, as several universal histories that predated Voltaire sought to take account of new forms of knowledge without entirely abandoning certain fundamental Christian truths. It is better, in other words, to think of Voltaire's work as an endpoint in a continuous process whereby the sacred was eventually displaced by the secular and profane.[53] And, indeed, there is no denying that Voltaire sought explicitly to reject the sacred in favour of the secular, as he stressed that his 'philosophy of history', as he called it, was emancipated from the theology of universal histories.

Significantly, Voltaire began his *Essay on Universal History* not with a discussion of Creation or with any reference to biblical events but rather with an analysis of China and ancient Chinese history. He did so because China's history could not be integrated into the biblical narrative. He also stressed the advanced state of Chinese civilization in comparison with ancient Israel. This suggested that there was nothing universal about sacred universal history. Any truly universal history needs to take into account the history of non-Western societies, whether or not they could be fitted into the biblical narrative.[54]

Although Voltaire rejected the providential meaning of sacred universal histories, his own universal history was not without an overarching theme.

---

[51] See Allan Megill's analysis of Bodin's critique of sacred universal histories in Megill, '"Big History" Old and New', 316–18.

[52] This interpretation largely originates with Hazard's *La Crise de la conscience européenne*.

[53] Griggs, 'Universal History from Counter-Reformation to Enlightenment', 219–47.

[54] Löwith, *Meaning in History*, 105–6.

With Voltaire universal history became a story of progress rather than of Providence. This understandably follows from the main ideals of the Enlightenment, of which Voltaire was a key figure, such as the use of reason to bring about self-improvement and happiness. For Voltaire, these ideals were themselves a product of the progressive direction of history. It is, however, a mistake to interpret this shift as a rejection of the Christian concept of history. As Karl Löwith (1897–1973) argues, it may be true that with Voltaire Providence was replaced by humanity, but the overarching conception of history did not change, as the 'Christian hope of salvation [had merely been secularized] into an indefinite hope of improvement and faith in God's providence into the belief in man's capacity to provide for his own earthly happiness'.[55]

If universal history threatened to become incoherent under Voltaire's comprehensiveness, other Enlightenment figures took a more philosophical and systematic approach. For example, in his 1784 essay, 'Idea for a Universal History with Cosmopolitan Intent', Immanuel Kant (1724–1804) sought to articulate a programme for how a universal approach to human history could be constructed in an enlightened and secular age. Kant argued that when viewed from the right distance, past human actions appear not as the result of chance but rather as the product of natural laws. In the same way that statistics uncover regularities that are invisible from an analysis of singular facts, something analogous can be discerned with reference to human history. Thus, Kant argued, 'What appears to be complicated and accidental in individuals, may yet be understood as a steady, progressive, though slow, evolution of the predispositions of the entire species.'[56] Kant admitted that such a law of human history had yet to be discovered, but he held out the hope that nature might produce someone capable of doing so in the same way that 'nature produced a *Kepler* who figured out an unexpected way of subsuming the eccentric orbits of the planets to definite laws, and a *Newton* who explained these laws by a general cause of nature'.[57]

Kant then proceeded to outline nine propositions that were to act as a general framework for what a universal history directed to uncover the laws of the human past might look like. What was centrally important for Kant was that such a universal history would need to focus on how reason developed not in the individual but in the species as a whole, and on how that reason was then put to use far beyond the level of 'natural instinct'. Such a universal history would then be a story of how the human species utilized its reason to overcome the

[55] Löwith, *Meaning in History*, 111.
[56] Kant, 'Idea for a Universal History with Cosmopolitan Intent', 117.
[57] Kant, 'Idea for a Universal History with Cosmopolitan Intent', 118.

antagonisms that confronted humans in an early stage of development and led to the creation of civil society. The moral of this story would be that history was still unfolding according to this law, which would end with the realization of a form of rational government that Kant envisioned as 'cosmopolitan'.[58] It was in this way, Kant wrote that 'the history of mankind could be viewed on the whole as the realization of a hidden plan of nature in order to bring about an internally – and for this purpose also externally – perfect constitution; since this is the only state in which nature can develop all predispositions of mankind'.[59] For Kant, the providential story of previous universal histories was to be replaced, quite literally, by a natural story, the outcome of which was to be presented as the result of the unfolding of natural processes established at the very beginning.

While Kant did not himself aim to produce such a universal history, it is not difficult to recognize his influence on subsequent attempts to do so. With the Marquis de Condorcet's (1743–94) *Outlines of a Historical View of the Progress of the Human Mind* (1793), for instance, we have a clear attempt to construct the naturalistic plan advocated by Kant and combined with the progressivism of Voltaire, but focused on the development of the human intellect. Composed during the French Revolution while he was in hiding from the Jacobins, Condorcet's *Outlines* was written in order to situate the present overturning of the established order within the framework of a universal history that would also act as a guide for future developments. Like his sacred history predecessors, Condorcet structured his history via a series of epochs that focused on particular stages of human development. But rather than focusing on the development of Christianity as the central subject of his universal history, Condorcet focused on the development of scientific ideas and rational principles. It was, moreover, not Providence that governed the history of the human species, according to Condorcet, but progress itself, which was driven by the accumulation of knowledge.

More specifically, Condorcet divided his historical analysis into 'nine grand epochs' that represented the main stages of intellectual development, with a tenth epoch that 'conjecture[d] upon the future destiny of mankind'.[60] Condorcet's history began with a discussion about when humans first must have banded together, as families sought larger groupings for the purposes of mutual benefit. This first epoch, which Condorcet entitled 'Men United into Hordes', witnessed the origins of language and science but also of tyranny and

---

[58] For a discussion of the complicated history of the cosmopolitan concept, see Penman, *The Lost History of Cosmopolitanism*, 120–4 (on Kant).

[59] Kant, 'Idea for a Universal History with Cosmopolitan Intent', 128–9.

[60] Condorcet, *Outlines of an Historical View of the Progress of the Human Mind*, 19–20.

superstition.[61] This set up a central antagonism in Condorcet's history between superstition on one hand and knowledge on the other, with the latter advancing throughout the epochs until superstition was eventually overcome, in the recent past, by the final embrace of a rational and scientific view of nature and humanity. This progressive story of the accumulation of knowledge is mimicked by Condorcet's own method, which embraced scientific principles of history at the expense of metaphysics; his task, therefore, was not to make philosophical pronouncements on the nature of the past but rather to 'arrange facts, and exhibit the useful truths which arise from them as a whole, and from the different bearings of their several parts'.[62]

The most central epoch for Condorcet was the eighth, marked by the invention of printing and by scientific advances represented by Copernicus and Galileo.[63] The printing press enabled dramatically increased accumulation of knowledge that then managed to break 'every political and religious chain[.]'[64] Moreover, during the eighth epoch fundamental knowledge of the cosmos and the world was established, meaning that knowledge of man himself within the context of the 'globe which he inhabits' became possible.[65] This process continued in the ninth epoch, represented by the rationalism of Descartes, the mathematical physics of Newton, and the 'Formation of the French Republic' of Condorcet's present. In this stage, reason and rationality were brought to bear on governance and the 'rights of man', and mathematical knowledge was applied to astronomy. It also just so happens that this was the epoch when it became possible to understand the history of humanity from a holistic and scientific perspective, and recognize what remained to be done in order to advance the progress of humanity into the future. 'It is by arriving at this last link of the chain', Condorcet argued, 'that the observation of past events, as well as the knowledge acquired by meditation, become truly useful. It is by arriving at this term, that men learn to appreciate their real titles to reputation, or to enjoy, with a well-grounded pleasure, the progress of their reason. Hence, alone, it is, that they can judge of the true improvement of the human species.'[66]

In the final, tenth epoch, the 'Future Progress of Mankind', Condorcet argued that this properly scientific understanding of the past of humanity makes it possible to glimpse 'with some degree of truth, the picture of the future destiny of mankind'.[67] That destiny, Condorcet claimed, would take three specific

[61] Condorcet, *Outlines of an Historical View of the Progress of the Human Mind*, 21–8.
[62] Condorcet, *Outlines of an Historical View of the Progress of the Human Mind*, 14.
[63] Condorcet, *Outlines of an Historical View of the Progress of the Human Mind*, 209–10.
[64] Condorcet, *Outlines of an Historical View of the Progress of the Human Mind*, 183.
[65] Condorcet, *Outlines of an Historical View of the Progress of the Human Mind*, 188.
[66] Condorcet, *Outlines of an Historical View of the Progress of the Human Mind*, 314.
[67] Condorcet, *Outlines of an Historical View of the Progress of the Human Mind*, 316.

forms: 'the destruction of inequality between different nations; the progress of equality in one and the same nation; and lastly, the real improvement of men'.[68] Condorcet believed that these areas of life would advance because his history had shown that progress itself is indefinite; indeed, the constant accumulation of knowledge is not just social but biological, transmitted from parents to progeny at birth. Sounding much like Kant, he argued that 'perfectibility' would come about as a product of the natural course of history.[69]

Positivist philosophies of history of the nineteenth century built on and refined Condorcet's approach, while largely jettisoning Condorcet's ten epochs in favour of three general stages of intellectual development. This was the central innovation of Auguste Comte (1798–1857), who posited that human development has gone through three progressive stages: the theological, the metaphysical, and the positivist. In the theological stage, human knowledge ascribed supernatural agency to natural events and processes, which led eventually to the creation of monotheistic religions. In the metaphysical stage, natural phenomena were deemed to be caused by abstract forces rather than by supernatural intervention, although religion remained central to the ordering of life. It was only in the positivist stage, which overlapped with Comte's present, that natural phenomena were recognized as being caused by laws of nature that operated without reference to a deity.[70]

It is important to recognize that Comte's positive philosophy was also a history of science, as he argued that the individual sciences go through these stages of development as well, although not at the same time. It was the physical sciences that first reached the positivist stage, defined by the articulation of the scientific method. This method, according to Comte, would eventually be adopted by the other sciences and would thus establish a grand unity of knowledge, culminating in the establishment of the science of sociology.[71] Comte contended that knowledge of all life, from the motion of the planets to the structure of society, would be systematised and synthesized, thereby enabling the rational organizing of society and the limitless progress that Condorcet earlier envisioned (and would be reformulated under the idea of 'consilience' by E. O. Wilson in the next century).

Comte also recognized, however, that religion provides a societal function that science needs to appropriate under the guise of what he called the 'Religion of Humanity'. This involved replacing the worship of religious figures with the great scientific heroes of Comte's history of science, which was most notably

[68] Condorcet, *Outlines of an Historical View of the Progress of the Human Mind*, 317.
[69] Condorcet, *Outlines of an Historical View of the Progress of the Human Mind*, 370.
[70] Comte, *System of Positive Philosophy*, vol. 1, 26.
[71] Comte, *System of Positive Philosophy*, vol. 1, 355–517; and Löwith, *Meaning in History*, 69.

expressed in the form of a new liturgical calendar that included 13 months of 28 days each. The months symbolized Comte's progression of knowledge, with the first called 'Moses', representing 'the initial theocracy', and the thirteenth called 'Bichat' (for French anatomist Xavier Bichat [1771–1802]), representing 'modern science'. Moreover, every day was devoted to the worship of a specific historical figure.[72] This complicated liturgical apparatus, which included a system of prayers and sacraments, led the English naturalist Thomas Henry Huxley (1825–95) to quip that Comte's Religion of Humanity was essentially 'Catholicism *minus* Christ'.[73] But for Comte, Catholicism provided an important social function that science had to appropriate in order to bring about the final, positivist stage of history.

In England, while Comte's Religion of Humanity received a decidedly mixed reception, his broad historical scheme for understanding the development of scientific knowledge was embraced by a cross-section of philosophical and historical thinkers, notably John Stuart Mill (1806–73) and Frederic Harrison (1831–1932).[74] For our purposes, it is the work of autodidact Henry Thomas Buckle (1821–62) that is most relevant. Inspired by Comte, Condorcet, and Kant, Buckle sought to write a universal history of the progress of knowledge in a book entitled *The History of Civilization in England*, that he envisioned in ten volumes, although his early death meant that he would only produce two (1857, 1861). His plan was to compare the development of knowledge or what he called 'civilization' in England with other nations in order to map out a natural course of history that would make possible the prediction of future progress.

For Buckle, in following from the views of his enlightened predecessors, Europe represented the pinnacle of civilizational progress. He sought to explain why this was the case, arguing that the physical environment of the northern hemisphere was favourable to intellectual development. Unlike in other parts of the world, where climate and geography made survival generally difficult, in Europe agriculture and the subsequent accumulation of wealth were enabled by favourable environmental circumstances, and knowledge was able to accumulate at a much faster rate. The subsequent different histories of European nations were then largely due to what Buckle, following Condorcet, identified as the battle between metaphysical and scientific spirits. England produced important historical figures who embraced the scientific spirit, whereas nations such as Spain and France were held back in their scientific development by the dominance of Catholicism.

[72] Comte, *System of Positive Philosophy*, vol. 4, 347–50.
[73] Huxley, 'On the Physical Basis of Life', 156. [74] Wright, *The Religion of Humanity*.

While Buckle's *History of Civilization in England* clearly represents an Anglocentric version of an already Eurocentric form of universal history, he believed that his results were due to his embrace of a scientific method of historical analysis. He therefore advocated making history into a science in the mould of physics. The universal historian, Buckle argued, following Kant, ought to aim to uncover the laws of historical development. Such laws, moreover, which were just as deterministic as those that govern the motions of the planets, could be discerned by analyzing statistical data that would elucidate the regularities of human history. It followed for Buckle that false doctrines, such as belief in chance or free will, were products of metaphysical thinking that needed to be overcome if history were to be brought to the level of other scientific disciplines.

Problematizing the turning of history into a science was Buckle's claim that historians do not have the kind of general knowledge that is necessary for producing the scientific history that he envisioned. He argued that historians had become too specialized, too obsessing with compiling minute facts concerning narrow subjects, while eschewing generalizations and large-scale analysis. 'The unfortunate peculiarity of the history of man', Buckle wrote, 'is that although its separate parts have been examined with considerable ability, hardly any one has attempted to combine them into a whole, and ascertain the way in which they are connected with each other.'[75] Buckle hoped that his own analysis of the laws governing the historical progress of civilization would convince other historians to follow his lead and embrace the project of attempting to combine the separate parts of history into a holistic narrative of historical progress. It did not.

While Buckle was not entirely alone in the mid-nineteenth century in seeking to synthesize the disjunct parts of history by uncovering laws of historical development, most contemporary historians bristled at his approach and promoted the supposedly narrow empiricism that Buckle derided. At roughly the same time Leopold von Ranke's methodological principles of history were influential in Europe. Those principles formed the basis of a very different science of history. For Ranke's chief English proponent, Lord Acton (1834–1902), who directed the first *Cambridge Modern History* (1901), history needed to be written by individuals with specialized knowledge of specific areas of study. It was important for the historian to adopt a method that would allow the facts to speak for themselves, something that was only possibly by focusing on a narrow subject with an identifiable set of facts. It followed that the kind of

[75] Buckle, *History of Civilization in England*, 3.

generalizing necessitated by Buckle's science of history was based on an outdated notion of genius that professionalizing historians largely rejected.[76]

In this way, David Christian is on to something when he says that 'toward the end of the nineteenth century, professional historians expelled universal history from the discipline'.[77] But Christian also suggests that universal history 'vanished' at this time, and only reappeared in the mid-twentieth century as the idea of producing a general history became popular again after the disaster of the First World War. While it is debatable whether or not historians actually stopped writing universal histories during this period, what Christian fails to recognize is the emergence of a related genre of large-scale history that was often written by scientists, science writers, and popularizers of science that came to be known as the 'evolutionary epic'. Big History's most immediate predecessor was not developed from within the discipline of history at all, but came from a genre of science writing that sought to produce just the synthesis of scientific and historical knowledge later advocated by Big History's practitioners.

2.3 The Victorian Evolutionary Epic

It is often remarked that Buckle's science of history was largely unsuccessful because he adopted physics as his scientific model for history, when there was a much more suitable science available in the form of evolution.[78] Buckle's work did pre-date Darwin's *Origin of Species* (1859) by two years, and so Darwin's careful treatment of what he called 'descent with modification' was unavailable as something that could feature in Buckle's scheme of universal history. However, Darwin did not invent evolution, and his work was itself predated by a much more immediately sensational account of evolution written by the Scottish publisher and science writer Robert Chambers (1802–71). Published anonymously in 1844, *Vestiges of the Natural History of Creation* not only put forward a theory of the transmutation of species, but also argued that the process of evolution is universal and could therefore serve the project of synthesizing all scientific knowledge.

What Chambers came to recognize was that recent scientific advances in astronomy, geology, and biology could all be seen in terms of what he called the 'development hypothesis'. This was a specific theory of evolution largely derived from Jean-Baptiste Lamarck's (1744–1829) notion of progressive development, which held that species change over time due to an inherent drive for improvement. For Chambers, evolutionary change is simply a natural result of growth itself.

[76] On the reception of Buckle and the development of an opposed, mechanical science of history, see Hesketh, *The Science of History in Victorian Britain*.
[77] Christian, 'The Return of Universal History', 12.
[78] See Hesketh, 'Without a Darwinian Clue?'

In the same way that an individual is born and then changes over time through maturity and old age, so does the species, which could also be understood as going through stages of development. Chambers likened this process to a universal 'gestation' of nature.[79]

As well as popularizing evolution, what was innovative about Chambers's approach was that he argued that his developmental theory reflected a fundamental unity of all life, meaning that it extended well beyond the biological to the geological and the cosmic. In making his case that 'the whole is complete on one principle',[80] Chambers wrote *Vestiges* in the form of a linear story beginning with the origins of the universe in a 'nebular fire mist' and ending with the future development of humanity. In between, he described the development of the Earth, the geological features of the Earth, and life on Earth, before focusing on a broad sweep of human evolutionary history. It was indeed a grand progressive narrative that Chambers believed was 'the first attempt to connect the natural sciences into a history of creation'.[81] He engaged in this endeavour, he explained, 'for the sole purpose of improving the know-ledge of mankind, and through that medium their happiness'.[82]

Making a case for transmutation in 1844, particularly as a unifying theory of nature, was a daunting prospect given the close association of transmutation with French working-class radicalism.[83] Chambers sought to overcome that problem by suggesting that his developmental hypothesis fit within the English tradition of natural theology. This tradition held that God's providential design can be discerned by uncovering the laws of nature, which were deemed a product of God's handiwork. This was a way to avoid the invoking of miracles in explaining natural phenomena, while at the same time suggesting that the entire purpose of science was to illustrate 'the Power, Wisdom, and Goodness of God, as manifested in the Creation', as was the remit of the popular Bridgewater Treatises of the early nineteenth century.[84] Chambers's case for the develop-ment hypothesis relied on this language, such as when he suggested that the developmental principle was 'in the first place arranged in the counsels of Divine Wisdom', meaning that God built into his initial act of Creation an evolutionary process that did not require further acts of intervention, as had been the expectation in the older theory of special creation.[85]

---

[79] [Chambers], *Vestiges of the Natural History of Creation*, 221.
[80] [Chambers], *Vestiges of the Natural History of Creation*, 359.
[81] [Chambers], *Vestiges of the Natural History of Creation*, 388.
[82] [Chambers], *Vestiges of the Natural History of Creation*, 387.
[83] See, for instance, Desmond, *The Politics of Evolution.*
[84] On the publishing and reception of the Bridgewater Treatises, see Topham, *Reading the Book of Nature*.
[85] [Chambers], *Vestiges of the Natural History of Creation*, 191–235, quote on 203.

Despite the book's popularity – it sold over 20,000 copies in just 10 years – the scientific consensus concerning its value was quite negative.[86] Some of the older devotees of natural theology, such as Adam Sedgwick (1785–1873), could not get over its unorthodox theism. Others, such as Huxley, who would later become a powerful advocate for evolution, found that the unnamed author simply did not have the requisite expertise to justify his attempt to formulate a scientific theory that could explain several different branches of science.[87] While the book's anonymous status protected the author and his family from the vitriol, it also meant that critical readers could project their own fears and desires onto the space left vacant by the lack of an authorial name.[88] Because of this harsh treatment, and because the theory at the heart of the book was rendered obsolete by Darwin's subsequent theory of natural selection, the book is often considered a scientific failure.

What this argument fails to recognize is the impact the book had on its many readers. It is true that subsequently Darwin's *Origin of the Species* produced a more careful (and narrower) treatment of evolution, but it is also true that *Vestiges* helped prepare the public to accept the idea of evolution in the first place. This was something Darwin admitted in his historical sketch of evolution that was included in later editions of *Origin of the Species*. And, most importantly, *Vestiges* helped establish an entire genre of science writing that sought to connect the cosmic, the geological, the biological, and the historical via a unifying scientific theory and romantic narrative.[89]

Big historian Fred Spier has recognized that *Vestiges* represents an early predecessor to the modern practice of Big History. He argues, however, that after *Vestiges* 'no new big histories were published' until H. G. Wells's (1866–1946) *Outline of History* in 1920.[90] Spier's assumption is that because history became more specialized during this period, the grand sweeping narratives represented by *Vestiges* would have vanished, which, as we have seen, is a similar assumption that Christian makes about universal history 'vanishing' during this period. But this is simply not the case, particularly when we look outside of the disciplinary boundaries of history and into the realm of science writing, where grand narratives of scientific development existed in abundance, influenced not just by *Vestiges* but by Darwin's theory of natural selection as

[86] On the popularity of *Vestiges*'s, see Secord, *Victorian Sensation*, esp. 526 for sales figures.
[87] There is an excellent analysis of Huxley's review in Bashford, *The Huxleys*, 61–3.
[88] On the reception of *Vestiges*, see Yeo, 'Science and Intellectual Authority in Mid-Nineteenth-Century Britain'.
[89] Lightman, *Victorian Popularizers of Science*, chapter 5.
[90] Spier, *Big History and the Future of Humanity*, 23–4, quote on 23.

well as by Herbert Spencer's (1820–1903) cosmic evolutionism and Wallace's spiritual Darwinism.[91]

The work of anthropologist and travel writer Winwood Reade (1834–76) is a case in point. Reade initially made a name for himself as a traveller in Africa, and because of this became a correspondent with Darwin. He furnished Darwin with a series of observations about African expression and beauty that Darwin incorporated into his studies of human evolution, *The Descent of Man* (1871) and *Expression of the Emotions* (1872). Subsequently, Reade was inspired by Darwin's work and sought to write, as he told Darwin, a Darwinian 'universal history'.[92] He wanted to show how Darwin's principle of natural selection had been at work throughout human history, with the hope of guiding evolutionary progress in the future. From Reade's perspective, human history is best understood as a series of immense struggles for existence.[93]

Reade was also influenced by Comte and Buckle, and this is most clearly evidenced in the tripartite structure of *Martyrdom of Man* (1872), which posited that humans had transitioned through three distinct stages of history represented by 'War', 'Religion', and the 'Intellect'. In the first stage of human history, development was largely dependent on constant wars between individuals and tribes. In the second stage, as tribes became larger for purposes of security, the threat of war decreased, which enabled the development of monotheistic religions such as Christianity. In the third stage, represented by the 'intellect', Reade argued that further development meant that religious and metaphysical views could be overcome by scientific conceptions of society and the universe. The impact of the Darwinian struggle for existence, therefore, had slowly declined over the years as each generation benefitted just a little from the suffering or 'martyrdom' of the preceding generation, hence the title.[94]

It is in the last section of the book, on the intellect, where Reade's Darwinian universal history becomes a full-blown evolutionary epic, indicating that Reade was also a reader of *Vestiges*. He argued it is possible to understand how the human intellect had evolved only if one situates human history within the context of the history of the cosmos. 'If we take the life of a single atom, that

---

[91] On Spencer's widespread influence, see Lightman (ed.), *Global Spencerism*; and on Wallace's spiritual Darwinism, see Hesketh, 'The First Darwinian'.

[92] Reade to Darwin, 12 September 1871, Darwin Correspondence Project, www.darwinproject.ac.uk/letter/?docId=letters/DCP-LETT-7936.xml&query=Winwood%20Reade (accessed 4 June 2022).

[93] On the development of Reade's evolutionary epic in relation to Darwinism, see Hesketh, 'A Good Darwinian?'

[94] Reade, *The Martyrdom of Man* (1872), 543.

is to say of a single man, or if we look only at a single group, all appears to be cruelty and confusion', Reade argued; 'but when we survey mankind as One, we find it becoming more and more noble, more and more divine, slowly ripening towards perfection'.[95] Reade explained how this was the case by describing the origin of all things in the nebular fire mist. He then described the origin of the solar system, the Earth, life on Earth, and the origin of the human species. The quick evolution of the human mind, moreover, indicated to Reade that humans had essentially overcome those natural processes that were responsible for their birth, a view also postulated by Wallace.[96] And he said that by understanding 'the method of nature's operations, we shall be able to take her place and perform them ourselves'. Reade also argued that such knowledge will allow us 'to predict the future as we are already able to predict comets and eclipses and the planetary motions'.[97] He would go on at the end of *Martyrdom* to make some rather uncanny predictions, such as the invention of automobiles and passenger airplanes. He even envisioned that humans would in the very near future be migrating to the inner planets of the solar system, thanks to the invention of space travel. Reade argued for these claims by situating his universal history of humanity within a cosmic framework.[98]

The book received an initially hostile reception because, unlike Chambers, Reade argued that Christianity represents a final barrier to achieving evolutionary perfectibility. Negative reviews followed, and subsequent evolutionary epics sought to situate humanity's evolutionary past and future within theistic perspectives.[99] Despite this opposition, Reade's *Martyrdom of Man* rose in popularity in subsequent years. From 1872 until 1912, it had reached about 20,000 copies. By the time of the First World War, the book had become a sort of secularist Bible, as it was reprinted by the Rationalist Press Association, appearing in a few different versions over the years. It was also translated into multiple languages. Between 1924 and 1948 the Rationalist Press edition alone printed 130,000 copies.[100] Given these figures, it should not be surprising that it had outspoken admirers, including such influential and diverse political and literary figures as W. E. B. Du Bois (1868–1963), Cecil Rhodes (1853–1902), Arthur Conan Doyle (1859–1930), George Orwell (1903–50), and, most notably, H. G. Wells.

---

[95] Reade, *The Martyrdom of Man* (1872), 521–3.
[96] See Hesketh, 'The Future Evolution of "Man"', 197.
[97] Reade, *The Martyrdom of Man* (1872), 513.
[98] Reade, *The Martyrdom of Man* (1872), 513–15.
[99] Theistic evolutionary epics from the late Victorian period include Butler, *Life and Habit*; George Campbell (Duke of Argyll), *The Unity of Nature*; and Drummond, *The Ascent of Man*. On the reception of Reade's *Martyrdom of Man*, see Hesketh, 'A Good Darwinian?' 50–1.
[100] See the figures listed on the copyright page of Reade, *Martyrdom of Man* (1968).

2.4 Evolutionary Epics in the Age of Global Catastrophes

For practitioners of Big History, H. G. Wells is an important precursor, largely because his *Outline of History*, published in 1920, situated a fairly detailed description of human history within the history of the cosmos. But perhaps equally important was the rationale Wells put forward to justify writing his large-scale history, a rationale that is also utilized by big historians. Wells wrote his *Outline of History* in the wake of the First World War, at a moment when the world was undone because of nationalist rivalries that had led a generation into the trenches. His *Outline of History* was therefore driven, as Christian has argued, by the same sense of human unity that drives Big History. And just like the big historians, 'Wells understood [that] a universal history is the natural vehicle for a unified history of humanity, because, unlike national histories, big history first encounters humans not as warring tribes, but as a single and remarkably homogenous species'.[101] This presentation of Wells as a peace-driven universal historian, however, obscures his deep investment in a theory of evolutionary struggle forged when he was a young man.

Wells had first gained popularity not as a universal historian but as an author of science fiction. He had a deep interest in biology that was initially cultivated at the Normal School of Science, where he attended classes taught by Thomas Henry Huxley. While Wells eventually abandoned the idea of making a career as a biologist, his fiction was informed by contemporary scientific theories, notably that of evolution. Indeed, his enduringly popular novel *The Time Machine* (1895) was an evolutionary epic that postulated a future existence wherein the class divisions of English society eventually led to the creation of two distinct humanoid species, the Eloi and the Morlocks. *The Time Machine* appeared when the theory of evolutionary degeneration was at its height, which was the view that in the absence of an intense struggle for existence, de-evolution would take place, a process that had allegedly been shown at work in the evolutionary history of crustaceans and sea squirts. Wells's friend and future collaborator, the biologist Edwin Ray Lankester (1847–1929), had even warned in his book *Degeneration: A Chapter in Darwinism* (1880) that humans were not necessarily excluded from this process, meaning that in certain circumstances they could end up just like their ascidian cousins.[102] This is exactly what Wells postulated in *The Time Machine,* which became all too apparent in the stunning revelation that the Eloi, who were descended from the upper classes, were being harvested by the underground Morlocks, themselves descended from the working classes. The message was that while humans may have become conscious of the

[101] Christian, 'What is Big History?' 19. [102] Lankester, *Degeneration*, 61–2.

evolutionary process, they need to understand what actually engenders progress in order to avoid such horrific decline and degeneration.[103]

This was also one of the key messages of Reade's *Martyrdom of Man*, which greatly influenced Wells's evolutionary thinking and stimulated his interest in combining biological knowledge and human history within the framework of a universal story of life. Moreover, the book became a model for his *Outline of History*. As Wells explained in the introduction, '[r]emarkably few sketches of universal history by one author have been written. One book that influenced the writer is Winwood Reade's *Martyrdom of Man*. This *dates*, as people say, nowadays, and it has a fine gloom of its own, but it is still an extraordinary presentation of human history as one consistent process.'[104] Wells thus sought to present his own version of 'human history as one consistent process', beginning with the cosmic origins of the universe, life on Earth, and development of human society and culture through to the disastrous 'war to end all wars'. He placed the blame on the catastrophe at the feet of the nineteenth century, which, he argued, too quickly removed the 'ancient restraints' of religion, which led to a '*de-civilization* of men's minds'. He believed that those restraints needed to be brought back, not in the exact form of religion, but rather as an 'educational reformation'. Such a reformation 'must ultimately restore universal history, revised, corrected and brought up to date, to its proper place and use as a backbone of a general education. We may say 'restore,' because all the great cultures of the world hitherto, Judaism and Christianity in the Bible, Islam and the Koran, have used some sort of cosmology and world history as a basis.' He then suggested that 'without such a basis any really binding culture of men is inconceivable. Without it we are chaos.'[105] For Wells, making universal history the centre of an educational reformation was necessary to avoiding chaos and the inevitable degeneration to follow.

An important part of this educational reformation was the message that Wells wanted to impart, namely, that under the proper guidance evolution could become a directed process. In this regard Wells was on the same page as the biologist Julian Huxley (1887–1975), the grandson of Thomas Henry Huxley. Wells and the younger Huxley often collaborated, even producing (along with Wells's son, G. P. Wells [1901–85]) a textbook on evolution that sought to impart this message to biology students. After carefully detailing the facts in favour of evolution by tracking the evolution of life from single-celled organisms to humans, the authors sought to explain how, from the perspective of

[103] For an analysis of the cultural influence of evolutionary degeneration, see Pick, *Faces of Degeneration*, esp. chapter 6.

[104] Wells, *The Outline of History*, vol. 1, vi.

[105] Wells, *The Outline of History*, vol. 1, vi.

humans, evolution could be envisioned as a purposeful process 'based on foresight and deliberate planning instead of the old, slow method of blind struggle and blind selection'. Unfortunately, the authors explained, this notion was not realizable, at least not yet, despite the fact that 'human knowledge and power have grown very marvellously during the last few hundred years'. This was because the vast majority of the world's population did not know this story.[106] Educating the masses about this process was deemed the key to making evolution a purposeful process.

If the catastrophe of the First World War was what convinced Wells of the need to educate the masses about humanity's capabilities, it was ecological catastrophe that began to motivate authors of evolutionary epics in the second half of the twentieth century. Julian Huxley, for instance, became an advocate for the 'conservation' of endangered species and ecological habitats in the face of unbridled economic and political development, a position he promoted as founding director-general of UNESCO (1946–8).[107] The stakes for his conservationism grew immensely after reading Rachel Carson's popular *Silent Spring* (1962), which detailed 'with devastating clarity' how pesticidal chemicals 'are now destroying the ecological pattern of the countryside'.[108] The following year, Huxley argued that trends like those postulated by Carson give insight into the very real existential threat posed by such human activities. 'We must', argued Huxley, 'make the world at large aware that the whole future of mankind is endangered.' This was important because 'if present trends continue unchecked man will become the cancer of the planet instead of the guide and director of its further evolution'.[109] For Huxley, the environmental problem needed to be handled in the same way as do other large-scale issues, namely by educating the masses about the special place humans find themselves, at the current stage of evolutionary history.

Huxley found the key for understanding humanity's place and role at the current juncture of evolutionary history the philosophy of Pierre Teilhard de Chardin (1881–1955). Teilhard de Chardin was a Jesuit priest and palaeontologist whose *The Phenomenon of Man* (1955) put forward a theory of mental evolution that Huxley found particularly attractive for thinking about the relationship between evolution, education, and the environment. Teilhard de Chardin's work led Huxley to insist that 'the new and central factor in the present situation is that the evolutionary process, in the person of mankind, has for the first time become conscious of itself'.[110] This notion

[106] Wells, Huxley, and Wells, *Evolution: Fact and Theory*, 245.
[107] On Huxley's conservation efforts, see Bashford, *The Huxleys*, 183–96.
[108] Huxley, 'The Future of Man', 9. [109] Huxley, 'The Future of Man', 16.
[110] Huxley, 'The Future of Man', 19–20.

of evolutionary consciousness essentially referred to what Teilhard de Chardin, following the Soviet biogeochemist Vladimir Vernadsky (1863–1945), called the 'noosphere', which represents a third phase of earthly development after the geosphere and the biosphere. Huxley interpreted the noosphere as a way of thinking about how a 'unitary organisation of ideas and beliefs' could be integrated throughout human society, thus 'covering of the earth's sphericity with a thinking envelope[.]' But Huxley stressed that utilizing the power of the noosphere 'will not happen automatically: It can only be achieved by a large-scale cooperative exercise of human reason and imagination'. Huxley became convinced that this was the only way forward and it was to be achieved by recognizing the progressive stages of evolutionary history that was 'now revealed by the labors of historians, archaeologists, and anthropologists'.[111]

In order to facilitate the utilization of the noosphere, Huxley advocated transforming the education system so that it would 'give an overall picture of the world we have to live in and of ourselves who have to live in it, instead of dishing up a curriculum in a series of separate "subjects"'. He argued that such an 'integrated curriculum' should give a broad sketch of life from a very early age, while 'the evolutionary-historical idea could provide a central core and the ecological idea could cover the branching interrelation of subjects, while the idea of science, art, religion, and literature as psychosocial organs would bring the sciences and humanities into partnership'.[112] Through such a transformation of education a general evolutionary perspective could be imparted on the general population, one wherein 'the ideas of possible improvement and the vast extent of unrealised possibility are implicitly and explicitly stressed'. It was in this way, Huxley argued, that 'education could become an efficient agency of further human evolution'.[113]

Ultimately, for Huxley, the central message to be imparted was that humans, having become conscious of the evolutionary process, must be made to realise their special place in the order of things. After being decentred from the scientific picture of life for so long, Huxley argued that this new perspective should show the unique power and duty that humans must now recognize and accept for the benefit of future life. 'To me,' Huxley concluded, 'it is an exciting fact that man, after he appeared to have been dethroned from his supremacy, demoted from his central position in the universe to a status of an insignificant inhabitant of a small outlying planet of one among millions of stars, has now become reinstated in a key position, one of the . . . trustees . . . of advance in the cosmic process of evolution.'[114] This is a remarkable reversal of the more

[111] Huxley, 'The Future of Man', 7.
[112] Huxley, 'The Future of Man', 18.
[113] Huxley, 'The Future of Man', 19.
[114] Huxley, 'The Future of Man', 21–2.

stereotypical message that is appropriated from the history of science about humanity suffering a series of dethronements due to the discovery of heliocentricity, deep time, and evolution.[115] Humans under Huxley's scheme were not insignificant at all, but actually the most significant species and therefore have a duty to use their knowledge to guide and protect the evolution of life into the future.

Huxley's anthropocentric message of duty, agency, and uniqueness became central to the evolutionary epic from the 1970s onwards, particularly once E. O. Wilson followed up Huxley's calls for educational reform with his advocacy of replacing traditional religious cosmologies with what he called the 'epic of evolution'. His promotion of 'sociobiology', a field devoted to analyzing human behaviour and history from an evolutionary perspective, led him to argue that religion itself serves a fundamental evolutionary need that was being overlooked in an age of secularity. He believed that ideally a materialistic understanding of life would replace traditional religious cosmologies. But this was only possible within the framework of a narrative, an epic, that would bring together the various sciences under the umbrella of a general theory of evolution. It was Wilson's view that such a communal cosmology would enable a more distant futurity for both humans and other species. He even suggested that had the dinosaurs been able to understand themselves in such a grand cosmic framework, 'perhaps they might have survived. They might have been us.'[116]

Since the late 1970s, a group of scientists, popular science authors, and educators have sought to heed Wilson's call for the construction of an epic of evolution that would ground their environmental advocacy in a mythopoeic conception of the evolutionary process.[117] A prominent example of this is Brian Swimme and Thomas Berry's *Universe Story* (1992), a narrative of evolution beginning with what the authors call the 'primordial flaring forth' and ending with the present and future evolution of humanity. Relying on a combination of Teilhard de Chardin and Wilson they argue that humanity has reached a crossroads in the present. The hope, of course, is that with the knowledge provided by the story about how, thanks to human evolution, the universe has become conscious of itself, an environmental catastrophe can be avoided by the embrace of new forms of living. But they also suggest the possibility of a truly horrific new geological era that they name 'the technozoic', a disastrous future engendered by a failure to curb the advance of industrial society. The stakes for this 'emerging story' are therefore incredibly high, which is why advocates of the epic of evolution have sought to bring this story into mainstream education, where it can train future generations to think about their existence in such

[115] I discuss the origins of the reversal of this history of science trope in Hesketh, 'From Copernicus to Darwin to You'.

[116] Wilson, *On Human Nature*, 197.

[117] See Sideras, *Consecrating Science*.

holistic terms, hopefully engendering a viable future for the human species. We will see that Big History, which emerged in the early 1990s in the hope of transforming the study of history, came to rely on much of the same mythopoeic rhetoric that characterizes this particular iteration of the evolutionary epic.

3 Big History in Theory and Practice

With Swimme and Berry's *Universe Story*, we have arrived at the moment when Big History as a specific field of research and teaching began to appear in Australian universities and elsewhere. Section 3 of the Element, therefore, examines more closely the intellectual development of Big History as it was envisioned and practiced by David Christian and his Big History colleagues and associates. It will be important to keep in mind how Big History is different from the large-scale forms of history and the narratives of popular science that have already been looked at, and how it is similar to them. For big historians, the key differences relate to the science that underpins the story, which aspires to be thoroughly up to date and modern. What this means for them is that Big History has the capacity to impart a clearer understanding of the processes governing history, and is thereby able to establish a more accurate timeline of the central historical events. At the same time, Big History seeks to preserve the function that previous universalizing histories sought to provide, namely, that of serving as unifying narratives that impart deep, cosmic meaning in the hopes of establishing more social cohesion. But because Big History is based on the discoveries of recent science, it has the added benefit of offering real solutions to the long-term problems that confront humanity.

However, we will see that while the particular facts that underpin the Big History narrative may be derived from recent scientific findings, the overarching scientific theories and the philosophies of science and history that govern the narrative are of a much less recent vintage. By looking more closely at the Big History narrative, this section will unpack some of the key assumptions upon which it rests. How is it possible, for instance, to synthesize the various sciences and related temporalities to produce a singular, universal story of life? What are the scientific theories that make such a synthesis possible, and how do they shape the narrative? How are the contingent issues of human history incorporated into a narrative governed by deterministic laws of nature? How are the existential challenges of the present, represented most notably by the Anthropocene, informed by the assumptions built into this modern origin story? And how will knowledge of this story enable the foresight necessary to chart a viable path forward for the future benefit of humanity? These questions are addressed in turn in Sections 3.1–3.5.

3.1 The Myth of a Single Historical Continuum

Given that the term Big History was coined by David Christian to refer to an innovative first-year history course that he began teaching at Macquarie University in 1989, it is important to recognize that the idea of Big History was engendered, at least in part, to address a perceived pedagogical need. Christian felt that because of the narrow specialization of history, as well as of other academic disciplines, his students were not being taught the big picture. But from the start Christian envisioned Big History as not just providing the big picture but as also engendering the kinds of questions that are typically associated with religions and ancient mythologies. As he explained in his 1991 article that sought to make a case for Big History:

> Big history encourages us to ask questions about our place in the universe. It leads us back to the sort of questions that have been answered in many societies by creation myths. This suggests that history could play as significant a role in modern industrial society as traditional creation myths have played in nonindustrial societies; but it will do so only if it asks questions as large and profound as those posed in traditional creation myths.[118]

Christian has expanded on this theme in subsequent publications, referring to Big History in his *Maps of Time* as a 'modern creation myth' and most recently as an 'origin story'.[119] But if we already have multiple origin stories and creation myths to rely upon, why should the discipline of history take on the function of these traditional meaningful narratives?

Part of the answer to this question has to do with the fact that Big History is premised on an assumption that the increasing secularization associated with modernity has led to a general global sense of dislocation and fragmentation. This is because the religious cosmologies that previously ordered society are apparently no longer hegemonic. In this regard, Christian often cites the work of sociologist Émile Durkheim (1858–1917) as an authority. Durkheim famously argued that a central feature of modernity was that of 'anomie', a general feeling of anxiety brought about by a breakdown of the values and order associated with traditional religious views. While the very premise of a general decline in religiosity relies on a narrative of secularization that is contradicted by many recent surveys,[120] Christian believes in contrast to this evidence that traditional

[118] Christian, 'The Case for "Big History"', 227.

[119] Christian, *Maps of Time*, 2; and Christian, *Origin Story*, ix–x, 9–12. It is worth noting that Christian now describes Big History as an 'origin story' to avoid the more narrow and even unscientific connotations that tend to apply to the 'creation myth' formulation that was more prominent in his earlier publications. They are virtually synonymous in Christian's usage, however, and serve the same rhetorical function, which is why I link them here.

[120] See Harrison, 'Why Religion Is Not Going Away and Science Will Not Destroy It'.

origin stories and religions no longer hold the power they once did and can no longer guide humanity in the future. This is precisely where Big History's grand evolutionary narrative of life comes in to the frame in order to provide just the kind of cosmic meaning required to overcome the social fragmentation produced by the secular, modern world.[121]

This is perhaps why big historians often present their own discoveries of Big History as moments of conversion.[122] For example, in the introduction to *Big History and the Future of Humanity*, Spier argues that his specialized Dutch education meant that he grew up with a fragmented and disconnected view of the world. His perception of the world changed dramatically, however, when he saw the famous earthrise images of the Apollo 8 mission in the 1960s. 'I experienced a shock that I had never felt before and never experienced since,' Spier admits. 'Within a second, it changed my perspective of Earth beyond recognition.'[123] But it was not until he came across Christian's Big History course in 1992 that he encountered the kind of general historical overview that he had been searching for, one that allowed him to connect the cosmic perspective represented by the earthrise images with his individual development.[124] Big History, Spier explains, 'has become a wonderful way of explaining how both my own person and everything around me have come into being'.[125]

For Christian, this is ideally the experience that readers and students will have upon learning about the Big History narrative. It is this experience that he imagines ancient peoples had upon learning about their own origins. In *Origin Story*, Christian speculates about the origin story of the recently discovered Lake Mungo people, who lived over 40,000 years ago in present-day Australia, and must have gathered around the lake and considered their own existence in the context of their surroundings.[126]

> As they talk about the stars, the landscape, the wombats and the wallabies, and the world of their ancestors, the teachers build a shared map of understanding that shows members of the community their place in a rich, beautiful, and sometimes terrifying universe: *This* is what you are; *this* is where you came from; *this* is who existed before you were born; *this* is the whole thing of which you are a small part; *these* are the responsibilities and challenges of living in a community of others like yourself.

[121] Not all big historians have such a binary view of science and religion. See especially Blanks, 'Science and Religion in Big History', 11–32, and the other essays in Gustafson, Rodrigue, and Blanks (eds.), *Science, Religion, and Deep Time*.

[122] Katerberg, 'Is Big History a Movement Culture?' 63.

[123] Spier, *Big History and the Future of Humanity*, xii.

[124] Spier, *Big History and the Future of Humanity*, xv.

[125] Spier, *Big History and the Future of Humanity*, xiii.

[126] Christian, *Origin Story*, 6–7.

Christian goes on to say that stories like the one he imagines were produced by the Lake Mungo people 'have great power because they are trusted. They *feel* true because they are based on the best knowledge passed down by ancestors over many generations.'[127] For Christian, these kinds of stories are necessary, for they fill an essential, human need to feel connected to society and to the wider world and beyond to the outer reaches of the cosmos. This is not unlike the argument used by E. O. Wilson and other proponents of the evolutionary epic, who argue that it is a scientific narrative of life that taps into humanity's desire for mythological cosmologies.

While Big History is presented as being similar to ancient mythologies, it is also importantly presented as being different in a fundamental way. It is different, and in this way uniquely built for the modern world, because Big History's authority is not based on scriptures or handed down stories, but rather 'on the global traditions of modern science'.[128] This is why Christian, Brown, and Benjamin's Big History textbook refers to Big History as a 'modern, *scientific* creation myth'.[129] It may provide the same function as do creation myths and origin stories, but it does so by appealing to the authority of modern science. But what exactly makes Big History scientific?

Big History is scientific because it is based on a synthesis of a range of scientific theories that have achieved paradigmatic status in the Kuhnian sense. In this regard, Christian often refers to three paradigmatic theories in relation to three scientific disciplines: the theory of the Big Bang for astronomy; plate tectonics for geology; and the theory of evolution by natural selection for biology.[130] Putting aside whether or not a Kuhnian understanding of paradigms and scientific consensus building is actually appropriate in this context (or is an accurate statement of how science actually works), what Christian and other big historians stress is that these scientific theories are actually commensurable with one another. Moreover, because they are also fundamentally historical in their explanation of the phenomena in question, there is an assumption that these natural histories can be synthesized under the framework of a unifying theory.

For big historians, this assumption is appropriate because it is one that is apparently shared with working scientists, namely, that the natural sciences themselves are based on a unified conception of nature. As Christian argues, 'Within the natural sciences the assumption of an underlying unity between the different disciplines is taken for granted.'[131] This is, however, a fairly bold statement that reflects a view put forward not by the scientific community at large but rather by those who tend to promote the mythopoeic potentialities of

[127] Christian, *Origin Story*, 7–8. [128] Christian, *Origin Story*, 9.
[129] Christian, Brown, and Benjamin, *Big History*, 4, emphasis added.
[130] Christian, 'What is Big History?' 10. [131] Christian, 'A Single Historical Continuum', 22.

the scientific enterprise. In this regard it is most commonly associated with Wilson, who argued that the sciences are 'consilient', meaning that they share a fundamentally unified conception of nature. This was a key premise for Wilson, because it meant that the ultimate goal of science should be the construction of an understanding of nature that could serve as the basis of a grand overarching theory of knowledge, thereby providing the philosophical basis for the construction of the evolutionary epic. It is not surprising that the same appeal to the consilient nature of science is at the heart of Big History's claims about the scientific nature of their grand historicizing endeavour.

The fact of the matter is that Wilson's notion of consilience is a highly controversial view that far from represents an underlying assumption about the unity of nature that is shared across the scientific disciplines. For a start, Wilson's own formulation of the idea is based on a misunderstanding of the origins of consilience as a goal of nineteenth-century science. It is true that the natural philosopher William Whewell (1794–1866) appealed to what he called a 'consilience of inductions' as a test for the viability of proposed scientific laws. However, Whewell's notion of consilience referred to the ability of those laws to explain related but previously inexplicable phenomena; it did not refer to an underlying conception of nature that transcended the disciplines.[132] Wilson's consilience has far more in common with Comte's positivism, which postulated that all knowledge will eventually conform to a singular scientific theory that will be able to explain all things. Such a view is not necessarily wrong, but it is also not as unproblematic as proponents of Big History suggest. Wilson relies not on a common sense view of nature that transcends the natural sciences but on a contentious and disputable philosophy of science.

It is important to recognize, then, that in claiming to be scientific, Big History is actually embracing a particular understanding of science based on a philosophy that imagines scientific knowledge developing in a progressive and cumulative fashion towards some sort of universality. While this is a philosophy of science that often gets disseminated in popular science literature, particularly in works of cosmology that seek a unifying and simplifying theory of life, or works of popular biology that promote a 'universal Darwinism', the idea that the sciences are somehow consilient, or even commensurable, is highly contestable. Indeed, by the end of the twentieth century, it was likely more common to find natural scientists arguing on behalf of the disunity rather than the unity of science.[133] That the sciences may be disunified, is not a proposition that is considered by big historians, no doubt because that

[132] For a compelling critique of Wilson's view of consilience, see Sideras, *Consecrating Science*.

[133] See, for instance, Galison and Stump (eds), *The Disunity of Science*.

would undermine the very idea of being able to produce a unifying narrative of life that is informed by an integration of the historical sciences. It is much better to think, as Christian does, that '[t]here now exist no serious intellectual or scientific or philosophical barriers to a broad unification of historical scholarship'.[134]

Here we come to the crux of Big History's appropriation of the 'unity of science'. It is belief in such a unity that enables Christian's 'broad unification of historical scholarship', and thus the integration of the three paradigms of scientific knowledge into a grand narrative of life, or what Christian calls 'A Single Historical Continuum'.[135] This is the scientific rationale for Big History's claim that it is possible to produce a unified historical narrative that begins with the origin of all things in the Big Bang and runs through to the origin of life and to the history of the human species and beyond. Because the natural sciences are commensurable, so this argument goes, it is possible to synthesize the vastly different timescales associated with cosmology, geology, biology, and human history, as well as to explain the vastly divergent phenomena thereof under the same theoretical framework. This is far more problematic than Christian admits, yet unless we are able to integrate the different scales of time and the divergent phenomena of nature there will be no possibility of constructing a 'single historical continuum'.

Just as being based on an ideal of scientific consilience separates Big History from traditional creation myths, so also Big History's ability to construct a linear and continuous timeline that purports to identify the key events of history distinguishes Big History from older forms of universal history. The ability to date accurately the events of deep time is a recent phenomenon. Biblical timescales became impossible to maintain at the end of the eighteenth and beginning of the nineteenth century, when fossil discoveries made evident both a geological and a human antiquity. One result of this was that any supposed events that had occurred before the establishment of written records had to be accorded a fair amount of temporal vagueness. Expanded timeframes made possible the acceptance of scientific theories that had previously been contentious, such as evolution; but uncertainty surrounding the age of the Earth, and other important events in the development of life, made understanding that process more difficult. For instance, when Lord Kelvin's (1824–1907) calculations for the age of the Earth suggested that the immense amount of time that Darwin thought evolution had within which to operate was reduced to just a hundred million years at a maximum, the slow gradualism implied in natural

[134] Christian, 'A Single Historical Continuum', 22.
[135] Christian, 'A Single Historical Continuum'.

selection became much less convincing.[136] Not until well into the twentieth century, when the mistaken assumptions underlying Kelvin's calculations came to be recognized, could the real immensity of geological and cosmic timescales be grasped.

Even then, it proved difficult to situate with any sort of accuracy those events that preceded written records. This was something Wells lamented in his *Outline of History*, which could only refer vaguely to when certain prehistoric events occurred, such as the origin of humanity, life, or the cosmos. The 'chronology of events' that Wells included at the end of his *Outline of History* illustrated this perfectly, as it began only with the founding of Carthage in 800 BC. As Wells explained, 'Chronology only begins to be precise enough to specify the exact year of any event after the establishment of the eras of the First Olympiad and the building of Rome.'[137] His failure even to attempt to refer to specific dates before the Roman period is a testament to the scientific deficiencies of previous forms of universal history. For Christian, Wells's chronology, or lack thereof, was symbolic of a 'fundamental chronometric barrier [that] confined empirical historical scholarship to a scale of several thousand years and in practice to the study of literate societies and their elites. Though nineteenth-century geologists had determined *relative* dates for many geological eras, *absolute* dates were unattainable.'[138]

According to Christian, this situation changed dramatically in the middle of the twentieth century, thanks to what he calls the 'second chronometric revolution'. This refers to the emergence of a range of radiometric dating techniques that enabled the precise dating of events of the deep past. By measuring, for instance, the rate of decay of Carbon-14 in organic materials, it became possible to calculate dates up to approximately 50,000 years ago, and this has been used to great effect by archaeologists to date key cultural developments and transitions of prehistory. Meanwhile, a similar process was utilized to calculate the age of rocks by measuring the decay of uranium, making it possible to estimate the origin of geological as well as cosmic events, such as the age of the Earth and solar system.

Consequently, the story of Big History can now be plotted on a timeline with fairly precise dates that signify key biological, geological, and astronomical events. As Christian argues, 'since the 1950s, it has been possible to create a timeline that is based on reliable absolute dates and extends beyond the appearance of writing, beyond even the appearance of our species, to the origins of the earth and the universe'. This means that 'we can [now] do prehistory,

[136] See Burchfield, *Lord Kelvin and the Age of the Earth*.
[137] Wells, *The Outline of History*, vol. 2, 605.
[138] Christian, 'The Return of Universal History', 18; see also Christian, 'What Is Big History?' 11.

palaeontology, geology, and even cosmology with the sort of chronometric precision previously confined to the study of human civilizations'.[139] Constructing an integrated and linear timeline has therefore been an important symbol of Big History's apparent scientific rigour, while providing a visualization of Christian's single historical continuum. And yet there is an interesting parallel to be made with the early modern practice of chronology which, as we have seen, was driven by the desire to assign precise dates to the key events of the Bible such as Creation, the Fall, the Deluge, and the arrival of Jesus and founding of Christianity. The timescales involved are understandably quite different, but Renaissance and early modern chronologists were confronted with similar challenges of integrating both natural and human events, as well as sacred and profane histories, in order to construct a universal narrative connecting the events of the deep past with the present and future. For Big History, however, the story begins not 6,000 years ago by an act of God but rather 13.8 billion years ago with the Big Bang, the first of eight key events that structure Big History's single historical continuum.

3.2 A Theory of Everything

Christian refers to these eight key events as 'thresholds'. They provide the main structure for the Big History narrative, stretching back to the origin of the cosmos and forward to the present and beyond. The eight thresholds are: (1) the Big Bang; (2) stars and galaxies; (3) new chemical elements; (4) the Earth and solar system; (5) life on Earth; (6) the human species; (7) agriculture; and (8), our currently proposed geological epoch, the Anthropocene.[140] There is also a projected ninth threshold that predicts possible future scenarios based on the trajectory established by the preceding narrative. While these thresholds are meant to refer to key turning points, they also represent distinct periods of time and in this sense are not unlike the days, stages, or epochs that structured the narratives of universal history.

Periodization is, of course, an important aspect of much historical writing, not just of the universal variety. As Daniel Woolf has shown, while periodization seems like a necessary historiographical tool to bring some analytical order to an inherently chaotic past, 'periods have always been in danger of reification', meaning that they can 'become essentialized, ontologized, and immoveable boxes . . . whose very rigidity constrains the meaning of events'.[141] While this is particularly obvious for such essentialized periods as 'medieval' and

[139] Christian, 'The Return of Universal History', 18.

[140] These are the thresholds as summarized in Christian's *Origin Story*, 13–14.

[141] Woolf, 'Historical Periodization'.

'ancient', it is perhaps more obviously the case with periods that are supposedly derived from ancient scripture or scientific theories. From Big History's perspective, what makes its thresholds not imagined constructs but representations of real historical processes and events is the fact that they are informed by two apparently incontrovertible laws of nature: the second law of thermodynamics and evolution.

The general structure of the Big History narrative is governed by the second law of thermodynamics. It may seem odd that Big History would be shaped by a theory of physics, but for Christian what is central about the second law of thermodynamics is that it governs the direction of all organic and inorganic processes. In his now famous TED talk, Christian illustrated this by showing a video of an egg being cracked open and scrambled. What soon becomes evident is that the video is actually being played in reverse, and the egg is being unscrambled and then poured into a cracked shell which then becomes whole again. Christian's point in playing the video in reverse is to show that this is not how nature works. We do not create eggs out of mush, but mush can be created out of eggs.[142] The second law of thermodynamics holds that the direction of change in an isolated system is towards mush or what is called entropy, a unit of measure that describes energy that is no longer available for work. From a cosmic perspective, what this suggests is that the energy in the universe is slowly transitioning towards entropy and therefore the universe is winding down, until a state of equilibrium will inevitably be reached, and all life will cease.

When in the mid-nineteenth century this theory was largely established, it led to much anguish because of what it suggested about the apparent purposelessness of life. When Darwin, for instance, came to the realization 'that the sun with all the planets will in time grow cold for life', he found it difficult to accept given the immense evolutionary process that proceeded this ignoble end. 'Believing as I do that man in the distant future will be a far more perfect creature than he now is', Darwin wrote in his 'Recollections', 'it is an intolerable thought that he and all other sentient beings are doomed to complete annihilation after such long-continued slow progress'.[143] Darwin was by no means alone in feeling this sense of purposelessness with regard to the evolutionary process; it led many to embrace Alfred Russel Wallace's view that evolution would continue in the afterlife.[144] However, when the cosmic

[142] According to Daniel Dennett, 'A standard textbook expression of the directionality imposed by the Second Law of Thermodynamics is the claim that you can't *un*scramble an egg'. See Dennett, *Darwin's Dangerous Idea*, 70.

[143] Darwin, *The Autobiography of Charles Darwin*, 92.

[144] Hesketh, 'The Future Evolution of "Man"'.

timescale expanded exponentially in the early twentieth century to several billions of years in both directions, such eschatological anxieties became less prominent, as it came to be recognized that humanity's evolutionary progress could continue into an exceedingly distant futurity. Moreover, evolution not only offered an existential compensation with regard to the eventual end of the universe, it also illustrated a central process of life's development that seems to work in opposition to the second law of thermodynamics.

Although the entropic direction of the universe sets the stage for the Big History narrative, Christian and other big historians also argue that there are moments when sudden new forms of complexity appear. These 'threshold moments' are ultimately governed by a general theory of evolution that envisages the creation of new forms of complexity *despite* the second law of thermodynamics. This was a key principle of Teilhard de Chardin's evolutionary cosmology that particularly impressed Julian Huxley, because it seemed to explain how evolution can counteract the destructive forces of entropy. As Huxley explained, what Teilhard de Chardin showed was that the evolution of life 'is an anti-entropic process, running counter to the second law of thermodynamics with its degradation of energy and its tendency to uniformity. With the aid of the sun's energy, biological evolution marches uphill, providing increasing variety and higher degrees of organization.'[145] For Huxley this was best exemplified by the fact that humans had evolved from an initial form of life to a being of higher intelligence able to understand that very process. While Teilhard de Chardin tended to argue that the evolutionary process is driven by some sort of vitalist, internal force, big historians have relied on a more mechanical and yet also more literary mode of explanation.

For big historians, new thresholds of complexity are reached because of the right combination of what they refer to as 'Goldilocks conditions'. This is a notion that Spier originally adapted from the commonly held view that the Earth represents a 'Goldilocks planet', meaning that it inhabits an area in the cosmos in relation to the sun whereby the conditions are 'not too hot and not too cold but just right' for the development of life. For Spier, thresholds of complexity are reached for analogous reasons, namely, that environmental conditions and circumstances come together in just the right sort of way for new forms of complexity to appear. While this may seem somewhat simplistic and overly reliant on the 'just-so' trope of fairy tales that Stephen Jay Gould (1941–2002) criticized as being central to the circular, adaptationist logic of sociobiology, big historians stress that it is merely a literary device that is used to help understand a very real process.[146]

[145] Huxley, *Essays of a Humanist*, 216. [146] Gould, 'Sociobiology', 530.

This claim tends, however, to be contradicted firstly by the language that Christian relies upon when describing the 'miraculous' way in which thresholds occur and secondly by the reduction of thresholds to an easily digestible formula. In terms of the former, we are told that every threshold is miraculous because of the way environmental circumstances seem to come together suddenly at just the right moment – in this way every threshold is 'magical', according to Christian – along with a certain set of biological, environmental, or cosmic ingredients, leading to the creation of something new. But, at the same time, in terms of the latter, thresholds are explained by reference to a rather simple formula of 'ingredients + circumstances = new threshold'.[147] For example, when Christian describes the origins of Threshold 2, which witnessed the creation of stars and galaxies following the Big Bang, he explains that this was the result of a combination of gravity and matter that were created by the Big Bang. Similarly, Threshold 4, which refers to the creation of our solar system, was the result of 'simple chemical molecules orbiting young stars, [which . . .] provided the building blocks for entirely new astronomical objects: planets, moons, and asteroids'.[148] The emergence of every threshold can be reduced to this similarly simple explanation, allowing for the creation of easily digestible tables of information that summarize the 'Eight Thresholds of Increasing Complexity' in recent Big History pedagogical materials.[149] Despite being so miraculous, thresholds prove remarkably simple to explain.

What makes the theory of 'thresholds of increasing complexity' a unifying theory of life is the addition of the concept of 'energy flows', as originally developed by the cosmologist Eric Chaisson. Chaisson has written extensively about cosmic evolution and has been a long-time supporter of the Wilsonian epic of evolution, and now of Big History. Chaisson posits that complexity emerged in the cosmos as a result of flows of energy that seem to counteract the ultimate entropic direction of the universe.[150] He argues that the Big Bang produced flows of energy that became available in both structured and unstructured forms. Given the right circumstances, these flows of energy can be put to work as they pass through structures, and this is what ultimately leads to greater forms of complexity. This process is particularly significant for Big History: big historians see it as being at work throughout the natural world in reference both

[147] See, for instance, the Big History Project, www.bighistoryproject.com; Christian, Brown, and Benjamin, *Big History*; and Christian, *Origin Story*.

[148] Christian, *Origin Story*, 61.

[149] See the table 'Eight Thresholds of Increasing Complexity', in Christian, Brown, and Benjamin, *Big History*, 6–7. See also the Big History Project, www.bighistoryproject.com.

[150] Chaisson, *Cosmic Evolution*.

to the relatively simple structures of the cosmos and to the more complex and layered structures of the Earth. But there is an important distinction between the cosmic and the biological: compared to the cosmos, the more complex forms of terrestrial life require a much higher rate of energy flows in order to avoid degeneration. This is because the organic world, unlike the inorganic, is constantly undergoing development, a seemingly endless cycle of birth, growth, and decay. Each new stage of complexity requires increasingly dense energy flows if complexity is to be maintained.[151]

This linking of Chaisson's idea of energy flows and complexity with the notion of 'Goldilocks conditions' forms the basis for the specifically scientific contribution that Big History brings to history in general.[152] As Spier explains, 'the "energy flows through matter" approach combined with the Goldilocks Principle may provide a first outline of a historical theory of everything, including human history. While this theory cannot, of course, explain everything that has happened, it does provide an explanation for general trends that have happened in Big History.'[153] But, it is one thing to link these overarching theories to the creation and development of the cosmos and quite another to do so with regard to the origin and development of human society and culture. Yet it is precisely this connection that big historians emphasize in order to establish a holistic – and continuous – account of all of history.

Moreover, despite claims to its scientific nature, Big History relies on much speculation in its connecting of the different stages of the narrative. This is most obvious with regard to the threshold moments themselves, which describe immense transitions whose origins we know with little certainty. While the Big Bang remains a highly contentious theory of ultimate origins, other thresholds prove equally difficult to explain in any way that can stand up to scientific scrutiny. Take, for instance, the origins of life, or Threshold 5. According to the Goldilocks Principle this is explained as resulting from the existence of complex chemicals, a certain rate of energy flows, the presence of water, and a habitable planet.[154] While these might give us some sense as to the kind of environmental conditions that life depends on, it does not by any means explain how life actually began. Because no evidence exists of the first organism, biologists have had to invent one, a hypothetical 'last universal common ancestor' or 'Luca', who would have existed 3.8 billion years ago or possibly

[151] Spier, *Big History and the Future of Humanity*, 54–61.

[152] Note that Chaisson has been critical of the way big historians tend to reduce certain scientific principles to 'wobbly' concepts like that of 'Goldilocks circumstances'. See Chaisson, 'Big History's Risk and Challenge', 89.

[153] Spier, *Big History and the Future of Humanity*, 67.

[154] This is according to Christian, Brown, and Benjamin, *Big History*, 7.

4.2 billion years ago, or perhaps even earlier. We don't know. We also really don't know how genuinely alive Luca would have been. But most likely, according to Christian, Luca would have existed 'somewhere in the zombie zone between life and nonlife'.[155] It is entirely understandable that our knowledge of early life would be so speculative, but this speculation sits awkwardly next to Big History's rather extravagant claims about its basis in chronological accuracy and scientific rigour.

3.3 Humans

This kind of speculation does not diminish as the focus shifts to the history of humans, with Threshold 6. Indeed, fully grasping the origin of humans proves to be as difficult as discerning the origin of life. We are told that the main Goldilocks condition enabling humans to appear was a lengthy period of evolution that led to the development of a species with finely tuned manipulative, perceptive, and neurological capabilities.[156] But when, exactly, humans first appeared in the past can only be estimated, and this estimation is largely based on the dating of other humanoid species that have been discovered in the fossil record. While we used to envision humans as the endpoint of a lengthy evolutionary procession of ape-like ancestors, that picture has become incredibly complicated in recent years, as discoveries of fossilized humanoid species have multiplied.[157] Discovering an origin of human life that can be reduced to a singular moment in time seems even less likely now than it did before the discovery of carbon dating. Given that Big History's claims to scientific status are based on accurate dating, it is difficult to see what this perspective offers that is any different from the more chronologically vague stages of transition posited by earlier authors of the evolutionary epic.

Notwithstanding these chronological and genealogical complications, the Big History story posits that a new stage of history began with the arrival of humans. Humans represent something fundamentally new in the evolution of life. Most notably, humans developed a unique capacity to learn, and to pass that knowledge on to others, meaning that knowledge could now accumulate rather than disappear with each generation. This is a process Christian calls 'collective learning', a result of the development of new kinds of communication, such as language and writing, which are capable of driving change because of the way in which they allow for the preservation, accumulation, and dissemination of knowledge across space and time. Moreover, the advent of collective learning is

155 Christian, *Origin Story*, 90.

156 According to Christian, Brown, and Benjamin, *Big History*, 7.

157 The year 2021 alone has led to a remarkable series of discoveries: https://edition.cnn.com/2021/12/22/world/year-of-ancient-human-discoveries-scn/index.html.

evidence for Christian that with humans, evolution moved beyond the realm of the biosphere and into Teilhard de Chardin's 'noosphere', meaning that the evolutionary process led to the creation of 'a single global realm of mind, of culture, of shared thoughts and ideas'.[158] As Christian explained in his TED talk, with the rise of collective learning it is as if all of humanity has been connected to a single, global brain.[159] And, according to Christian, thanks to the collective learning process 'one tiny part of the universe is beginning to understand itself'.[160] The emergence of Big History as the scientific origin story of humanity is perhaps the most prominent example of this universal self-awareness unleashed by Threshold 6.

It is unclear just how this message about human self-knowledge and agency coheres with the universal theory of history that Big History employs. When applied to human development, for instance, the 'energy flows leading to greater complexity' theme does not lend itself well to an analysis of the contingencies of human history. This is apparent as soon as humans enter the narrative and begin to take advantage of their learning capacities by embracing an agricultural way of life. A well-worn trope of prehistory is that humans eventually abandoned the hunter-gatherer lifestyle that defined the early development of human life in favour of farming, which enabled establishing larger communities, thus paving the way for the advent of many aspects of modern society. There is no question that the shift to agriculture occurred in various parts of the world during a certain general timeframe; but debate has raged about when exactly that shift occurred, just how extensive it was, and what caused it to occur in the first place.

For Big History, the adoption of agriculture is understandably a significant turning point in its overall narrative, represented by Threshold 7. However, many of the issues that anthropologists and historians find interesting about the subject are largely irrelevant to the story constructed by Big History. What does matter, according to this story, is how the adoption of agriculture can be informed and explained by the scientific architecture that makes up the Big History approach. For instance, in Christian's *Origin Story* Threshold 7 is explained as having been brought about by a series of environmental and biological preconditions. Warmer climates, for instance, made growing wheat and other grains and cereals viable. Population increases meant that there were available hands and bodies to engage in the laborious tasks of farming. And the advent of certain technological innovations made adopting large-scale

[158] Christian, *Origin Story*, 172.

[159] Spier refers to this 'single global brain' as well: Spier, *Big History and the Future of Humanity*, 272.

[160] Christian, *Origin Story*, 157.

agriculture a viable prospect. Having set out the preconditions for the adoption of agriculture, however, Big History is largely at a loss to explain how or why it actually occurred. Christian suggests that the development of agriculture was largely driven by an inherent desire for energy flows, which from this perspective comes across as an internal drive built in to the processes of evolution.[161] But this explanation seems to be more informed by the logic of Big History's 'theory of everything' than it is by the actual known facts of the matter.

Indeed, recent studies of the period in which agriculture arose and spread, many of them synthesized in James C. Scott's *Against the Grain* (2017), present a much more complex picture, one that problematizes the notion that the adoption of agriculture was some sort of evolutionary or developmental necessity. By all accounts, the adoption of agriculture was a brutalizing affair that for a time only benefitted the few at the expense of the many. There is evidence, therefore, that cultivation of the land became a central dimension in multiple struggles for power, with large groups of nomads resisting it in order to preserve their way of life. Moreover, as David Graeber and David Wengrow point out, the very idea of an 'Agricultural Revolution' can no longer be supported by the archaeological evidence. 'In the Fertile Crescent of the Middle East, long regarded as the cradle of the "Agricultural Revolution", there was in fact no "switch" from Palaeolithic forager to Neolithic farmer,' argue Graeber and Wengrow.[162] The supposed switch took 'as much as 3,000 years after the cultivation of wild cereals first began', a lengthy period of trials and errors, struggles and defeats, that necessarily challenges any simplistic understanding of a sudden transition to agricultural society.[163]

It is not as if some of these details are completely ignored by big historians. In their textbook, Christian, Brown, and Benjamin do refer to the fact that farming was not by any means easier than the alternative. The work of cultivation was brutal and demanding and would have taken a great deal of foresight to adopt, even as its promoters would have known full well that the immediate future would be difficult. But in the final analysis these details are basically meaningless to the overarching narrative, as the various contingencies involved in the adoption of agriculture are ultimately irrelevant to the deterministic forces represented by a changing climate and increasing population densities.[164] As Spier maintains again and again when explaining the development of any seemingly progressive innovation in his *Big History and the Future of Humanity*: 'Apparently, the costs of all these new forms of complexity did not

[161] See also Spier, *Big History and the Future of Humanity*, 225.
[162] Graeber and Wengrow, *The Dawn of Everything*, 248.
[163] Graeber and Wengrow, *The Dawn of Everything*, 233.
[164] Christian, Brown, and Benjamin, *Big History*, 106–7.

outweigh their benefits.'[165] At some point, in other words, farming became more viable and necessary than the alternatives.

Part of what is happening here is this: the often irrational and unpredictable activities of humans are being fitted into a deterministic formula that was originally developed to describe the large-scale processes of nature. For Big History to make any sense at all, it is obliged to show that the same cosmic processes that originated with the Big Bang also function at the level of human history. But once the narrative shifts to human history, the analysis that big historians offer is forced to take place almost entirely at the level of analogy. In *Maps of Time*, for instance, Christian is at pains to show how the development of cities followed a similar process as does gravity, suggesting that people in the surrounding areas were pulled towards the denser urban core. But while gravity may be useful for making a vivid point in this case, the law of gravity has nothing to do with urbanization. Christian recognizes this, and even points out that the processes in question are analogous, not the same, but he then proceeds to insist that the analogy likely indicates some deeper connection.[166]

Similarly, in *Big History and the Future of Humanity*, Spier compares the social organization of agricultural societies with the development of multicellular life.[167] Apparently, '[t]he increasing interdependence of cells within multicellular organisms as well as their emerging inter-cellular division of labor was paralleled by growing human interdependencies and an emerging social division of labor'. For Spier, this is a 'striking parallel', but it is also presented as more than just a parallel, for Spier wants the reader to imagine that the same natural process of inter-cellular division is what leads to human divisions of labour. The theory that increasing energy flows lead to greater complexity underwrites the describing of a series of analogous (though different) astronomical, geological, biological, and human processes as being one and the same.

Much of this process of what we might call the 'determinization' of history is accomplished simply by describing human events in the terms of Big History's specialized discourse of Goldilocks circumstances, increasing complexity, and energy flows. In his discussion of Julius Caesar's conquering of Rome in the Gallic Wars, Spier pulls back the curtain to show how this is done. Whereas Caesar described the Roman victory as the result of a brutal war of attrition, Spier describes the war in the language of energy flows. It was, according to Spier, 'a struggle for domination consisting of efforts to change important

[165] Spier, *Big History and the Future of Humanity*, 271.
[166] Christian, *Maps of Time*, 291–2. For the criticism of Christian's over-reliance on analogy, see Frank, 'Universal History', 87–8.
[167] Spier, *Big History and the Future of Humanity*, 232.

prevailing circumstances in one's own favor, while seeking to destroy the other party's complexity either by outright killing or by destroying both its matter and energy flows and its Goldilocks circumstances'. As the Romans ended up surrounding the city of Alesia, and in failing to take the city by force decided instead to starve the city's inhabitants, what they were actually doing was cutting off the supply of matter and energy, thereby destroying a 'Gallic independent complexity'.[168] The war is therefore best understood as a struggle between competing forms of complexity whereby the Goldilocks conditions of one society became the target of another via the means of reducing energy flows (e.g., killing or starving).

It is beside the point whether or not an adoption of this language actually gives us more insight into what actually happened. The more important point to make is that reliance on this language (and on the formula it is based on) reduces issues of motivation and causation to impersonal processes that are remarkably distant from the historical actors involved. What results are bizarre formulations in which general Goldilocks conditions and the drive for denser energy flows are deemed responsible for any and all human endeavours. For example, Spier argues that the Goldilocks conditions that were created by the domestication of animals 'facilitated an increasing transmission of infectious diseases from animals to humans which, in turn, stimulated efforts to cure both humans and animals from the new sickness'. So, it was not a specific group of individuals who became invested in studying disease but rather disease itself that 'led to the emergence of both human and animal medicine'.[169] It may be true that without disease and sickness we would have no need for medicine, but it does not follow that disease itself gave us medicine. It could be argued that what Spier is really implying is that because of collective learning, the development of medicine was inevitable once infectious diseases became a significant problem that threatened to undermine the Goldilocks conditions of human life. But again we confront the problem of understanding how the particular human innovation occurred. The fact of the matter is that from the perspective of Big History we do not have to know anything about the details concerning how 'it' actually happened (whatever it was), because the Big History formula provides a ready-made explanation devoid of the messiness that comes when we examine the actual contingencies of history.

It is in this way that Big History, like other forms of large-scale universal history, is ultimately deterministic, and consequently has difficulty dealing with issues of contingency, particularly as they relate to human agency. This is not to

[168] Spier, *Big History and the Future of Humanity*, 218.
[169] Spier, *Big History and the Future of Humanity*, 237–8.

suggest that determinism should be rejected out of hand. As Allan Megill makes clear, any attempt to seek out deeper structures of historical causation is going to have to embrace some form of determinism. But there needs to be a recognition that this is necessarily in tension with the contingencies that work to challenge overarching theories. Megill's point is not that determinism should be rejected in favour of contingency, but rather that the tension between them needs to be acknowledged. And, ideally, that tension will be made a central dimension of a methodologically sound historical analysis.[170] It is precisely this tension that Christian dismisses when he claims that all difficulties that stand in the way of a unifying theory of history are institutional and conventional rather than empirical, intellectual, and philosophical.

3.4 Welcome to the Anthropocene

This problem of determinism and contingency becomes more pronounced as the narrative approaches the more recent past, or Threshold 8. In some ways this is the most important threshold in the Big History narrative, for it embraces the last few hundred years when human development (economic, geographic, demographic, etc.) expanded to such an extent that it has had a significant impact on the natural processes of the Earth. This is important from the perspective of Big History because, as big historians like to suggest, we cannot really understand the nature of that impact without understanding how humans are connected to biological, geological, and cosmic processes, and this requires situating humanity within the cosmic story of life. As the Big History narrative approaches the more recent past, therefore, the seemingly disparate astronomical, geological, and biological processes come together as human development is shown to be a product of them. But humans have also developed to such an extent that they are challenging the limits of those very processes. In the language of Big History, the drive for greater and greater forms of complexity is threatening to alter the Goldilocks conditions that made human life possible in the first place.

Here Big History is particularly aided by James Lovelock's (1919–2022) Gaia theory, which postulates that the many Earth systems are actually highly integrated and work together to create just the right balance, one that was central for the development of life. Previously, our understanding of the Earth's processes was typically not integrated, meaning that we did not recognize how an impact on one process of the biosphere can lead to changes in a seemingly separate process. Lovelock's contribution was to argue that it is necessary to understand that life on Earth is part of an entirely holistic system.

[170] Megill, 'Histories Unresolving Tensions'.

For much of the Earth's recent history, according to Lovelock, the Earth was able to adapt and adjust to various pressures, whether exerted by the dominance of one species or by environmental changes. But now, Lovelock insisted, humans are exerting such a pressure on the system that it is becoming unbalanced, leading to a host of related problems. What Big History appropriates from the Gaia theory, is the idea that the Earth and the life that it supports form a system that human development has decidedly ruptured, and a clear symptom of this is the dramatic altering of the Earth's climate. Indeed, attempting to shed light on the relationship between human development and climate change has been a central rationale for the necessity of establishing Big History.[171]

In recent years, this dimension of Big History has been further bolstered by the advent of the notion of 'The Anthropocene', which is a newly proposed geological epoch that is currently being debated by the International Commission on Stratigraphy. This naming of a new geological epoch is significant because it is a recognition that we are no longer living in the stable environment that defined the Holocene epoch, which refers to the previous 11,000 years when human social and cultural development flourished. While the decision to name and identify a new geological epoch rests largely with geologists, the Anthropocene is an idea that has been embraced by scientists and humanities scholars of various kinds, who have been attracted to it because of how it draws attention to the singular impact that humans have had on the Earth, from the reduction of biodiversity and the rise of greenhouse gases to an increase in average temperature and a dramatic increase in catastrophic weather events. Given that human impact can be considered from a variety of different disciplinary perspectives, there are many different interpretations of what the Anthropocene means and how it should be employed as an analytical and temporal category.[172]

One contentious issue surrounds the precise dating of the transition from the Holocene to the Anthropocene. The Geologists at the Stratigraphy Commission prefer dating the Anthropocene from 1950, as this is the moment when it becomes possible to visualise the impact of human activity on the geological record via a strata of plastics and other 'human-made minerals' that have become embedded in the Earth's crust.[173] This also correlates to the start of what has been called 'The Great Acceleration', when capital and industrial development rather suddenly expanded due to the processes of globalization

[171] See, for instance, Christian, 'The Case for "Big History"', 226; and Christian, *Maps of Time*, 8.

[172] A very useful introduction to the divergent disciplinary meanings of the Anthropocene can be found in Thomas, Williams, and Zalasiewicz, *The Anthropocene*.

[173] Thomas, Williams, and Zalasiewicz, *The Anthropocene*, 56–7.

and decolonialization and when a variety of climate indicators rather suddenly increased, such as greenhouse gases and biospheric degradation.[174]

For others, however, establishing 1950 as the moment of transition fails to appreciate the fact that many of the anthropogenic processes that spiked at that time began well before the mid-twentieth century. The invention of the steam engine at the end of the eighteenth century, for instance, which set the stage for the Industrial Revolution and much of the environmental pollution to follow, is often considered a symbolic moment of transition. Others want to push the date back even further in time to the so-called Agricultural Revolution, when humans began radically altering parts of the landscape. This temporal debate is indicative of different disciplinary approaches to dating.

For their part, big historians have embraced the Anthropocene as representative of the most recent Threshold, which is also referred to as the 'Modern World'. Given Big History's rhetoric of accurate dating, it is curious that its practitioners are not terribly fussy about the exact timing of Threshold 8, although none of the Thresholds reflect the temporal precision supposedly enabled by modern chronometric techniques. What matters for big historians about the Anthropocene is that it reflects the period of human history that overlaps with industrialization and globalization, during which the human species began to transform the Earth's biosphere in an unprecedented fashion.[175] This is also the period when mass democracy was established, when the 'Rights of Man' were posed and unevenly applied after often violent and constant struggle, when war became a totalizing force, when the globe was colonized and subsequently decolonised, and when large-scale acts of genocide were perpetrated on indigenous peoples and other minority groups, such as the systematic execution of 6 million Jews by the Nazis during the Second World War. How does Big History handle this transformative period in human history?

On one hand, the Big History formula seems to work well when describing the large-scale development of human activity during this era. When the Industrial Revolution is framed as a transformative shift away from one regime of energy (based on renewable power such as wind and water) to another (based on fossil fuels), the theme of increasing complexity at the cost of ever greater demands for energy flows makes a great deal of sense. Modern human societies have come to rely on the energy provided by fossil fuels, and demands for further economic and social development (i.e., greater forms of complexity) have up to now overwhelmingly necessitated seeking out and exploiting those

[174] Thomas, Williams, and Zalasiewicz, *The Anthropocene*, 53.
[175] Christian, *Origin Story*, 157.

non-renewable energy sources. The demand for greater amounts of matter and energy also played a major role in overseas expansion and colonization, wars and rebellions, and eventually globalization. There is no question that modern history is largely incomprehensible without understanding how the harnessing and subsequent drive for energy led to an integrated global landscape. That global integration requires ever increasing amounts of energy to support the world's current eight billion human inhabitants. To put these increasing energy demands into context, Christian points out that 'since 1800, the number of humans increased by more than six billion. Each additional human had to be fed, clothed, housed, and employed, and most had to be educated. The challenge of producing enough resources in just two hundred years to support an extra six billion humans was colossal.'[176] Up to now, the energy demands continue to grow in order to support the ever-expanding complexity of the human population, which continues to increase.

On the other hand, the Big History formula proves to be far too overdetermining when the analysis shifts from economic to social and cultural developments. Issues central to gender and women's history prove to be particularly problematic if we try to make them conform to a theory of everything derived from physics. For example, Spier argues that 'industrialization led to more equal rights between the sexes, because it hardly made a difference in terms of physical strength whether it was a man or a woman who pushed buttons on machines or drove cars'. Apparently, all women needed to do to receive the same rights as men was get a job, something that the increasing demand for new forms of energy made necessary. Doubling down on this analysis, Spier argues that industrialization also led to '[t]he invention of far more efficient ways of controlling human sexual reproduction [that] greatly contributed to strengthening this trend [of equal rights]. All of this allowed women to enter the public domain.'[177] So not only did industrialization lead to equal rights, it also afforded women the ability to control reproduction.

It could be argued that Spier's foray into gender history is not an accurate reflection of the Big History approach in this area. However, the same reductionism is also found in Christian's studies of Big History. In a mere three pages in *Origin Story*, Christian breathlessly describes the last 200 years of social and governmental transformation as being a product of 'the new energy flows and technologies of the Anthropocene'. This new 'energy flows' regime was central to the development of industrial capital, Christian argues, which in turn led to new systems of government that

[176] Christian, *Origin Story*, 266. [177] Spier, *Big History and the Future of Humanity*, 270.

> had to become involved in the day-to-day lives of all their citizens. This is because wage earners, unlike peasants, cannot survive without governments. . . . A specialist wage earner, like a nerve cell [another analogy!], cannot survive alone. This is why a world of wage earners is much more tightly integrated than a world of peasant farmers. Modern governments regulate markets and currencies, protect the businesses that provide employment, create mass educational systems that can spread literacy to most of the population, and provide the infrastructure for the movement of goods and workers.[178]

This process also led to the creation of mass democracy, widespread nationalism, the mass mobilization of society, the total wars of the twentieth century, and eventually the creation of more global institutions of governance such as the United Nations and the International Monetary Fund.[179]

Entirely missing from the analysis is any sense as to how these changes in governance actually occurred. Instead, these dramatic alterations are presented as if they were the naturally occurring results of the new regime of energy flows that was established with the Anthropocene. In the same way that Spier sees advances in gender relations as a consequence of the rise of industrial capital, Christian argues that mass democracy was simply a natural outcome of wage labour. The feminist and labour movements play no role in this story, nor do the struggles to overthrow colonial regimes, or the attempts to establish alternative forms of governance. The closest Christian comes to assigning any sort of agency is in reference to modern 'governments' that seem to act merely to do whatever is necessary to enable the energy flows logic of the Anthropocene to unfold in accordance with the law of increasing complexity. It goes without saying that this perspective is about as far away from 'the history from below' tradition of social history as is possible, but it is also incongruent with the ultimate message that Big History seeks to impart in the expectation of a future Threshold that needs to be shaped not just by deterministic laws but also by people.

3.5 The Quest of the Future

The Big History narrative concludes not with an analysis of the present but rather with a prediction about the future. Big historians like to point out that this aspect of the narrative is one of the ways that Big History is set apart from disciplinary history, which typically avoids speculations about the future. We are told that for Big History a discussion of the future is an entirely natural and acceptable conclusion given that the narrative has followed the path of life going back 13.8 billion years.[180] As we have seen, a futuristic conclusion is

[178] Christian, *Origin Story*, 268–9. [179] Christian, *Origin Story*, 269–70.
[180] See, for instance, Christian, *Future Stories*, 6–11.

a necessary dimension of universal histories, which typically use the wondrous knowledge uncovered by their narratives in the service of going beyond the current stage or threshold. This is where the reader is invited to take part in the collective journey described in the universalizing narrative of the past, by helping to bring about the future progress to which the narrative gestures.

Also, as with other universal histories and evolutionary epics, this is where the underlying normative rationale for producing the story is made apparent. As Spier explains in his concluding chapter on 'Facing the Future', 'many big historians are, in fact, motivated to write these long histories at least partially because they are worried about precarious aspects of future developments'.[181] Christian concludes his TED talk with a similar invocation of a precarious future, and an explanation that what concerns him most is the kind of world that will be inherited by his grandson. From this perspective, the story of Big History is meant to provide the kind of knowledge required to confront the large-scale challenges that face humanity as a whole. While Big History may be presented as apolitical, and as an entirely objective and scientific analysis of the past, these claims mask the fact that it is, as William Katerberg has argued, a 'movement culture'. That is, it seeks to challenge the status quo through the creation of an oppositional worldview that will help to bring about a new cultural formation.[182]

This becomes most clear in Big History's predictions, which end up looking less like descriptions of a future that is fated to come and more like normative directives. While it is true that the Big History narrative ultimately ends once the energy unleashed by the Big Bang has been expended, or perhaps when life on Earth is finally annihilated by the excess radiation given off by an expanding sun, humanity itself could continue for at least several million years. That long-continued existence, however, is threatened by unchecked human development that may well engender a sixth great extinction event and could lead to an apocalyptic scenario that either brings about the end of human life or at best makes human life more difficult. There is nothing terribly new or insightful about this vision of the future, as it was widely circulated in the 1970s in the form of the Club of Rome's *The Limits to Growth* (1972) and many environmental studies since that time.[183]

Spier was greatly influenced by *The Limits to Growth*, and closely followed its model of considering population growth and food and industrial production in relation to the Earth's quickly depleting resources. While some of the book's initial speculations proved to be off the mark, Spier argues that the authors'

[181] Spier, *Big History and the Future of Humanity*, 295.
[182] Katerberg, 'Is Big History a Movement Culture?'
[183] Meadows et al., *The Limits to Growth*.

claim that the Earth's capacity to support human life will be reached sometime in the late twenty-first century is proving to be quite sound.[184] Spier suggests a series of actions that must be taken in order to avoid this precipitous collapse in the current way of life, including keeping population growth in check, developing renewable forms of energy, limiting phosphate loss, as well as diversifying crops.[185] For Spier, these issues are interrelated: they all have to do with how humans have used energy to increase the complexity of human society, energy that is now too costly to utilize. But even moving towards a new energy regime in order to preserve human life in the future will necessitate an initial reduction in complexity that will ultimately benefit future generations. Passing through this bottleneck, will require everyone to unite and accept responsibility for making difficult decisions. 'Successfully passing through this expected bottleneck will require unprecedented global cooperation,' Spier argues, 'which can only be achieved when sufficient numbers of people are aware of this situation and feel they have a personal interest in trying to make this transition as smoothly as possible.' Ultimately for Spier, this is the purpose of Big History, to show humanity how it is possible to 'use its global brain for achieving global cooperation'.[186]

Christian's discussion of the future in *Origin Story* is roughly similar. Christian presents two plausible scenarios regarding humanity's near future, based on the Big History narrative. Following from recent futuristic discussions of the Anthropocene, he considers these two scenarios alongside the notions of the 'Good Anthropocene' and the 'Bad Anthropocene'. For Christian, the Good Anthropocene refers to all the genuinely good achievements that have come about thanks to the globalization of industrial capital, such as the rise of life expectancy and democracy. The Bad Anthropocene refers to the many negative aspects of life that have been engendered, such as rising inequality and environmental degradation. Should human activity continue along its current trajectory, Christian worries that the Bad Anthropocene will become more prominent and that human life will become more difficult. He hopes, however, that there will be ways to preserve the positive aspects of the Anthropocene while the negative ones are reduced, leading to a more equitable and environmentally harmonious future.[187]

This latter scenario is less a prediction than a challenge or 'quest' that Christian argues humanity must accept if the 'morally unacceptable' world of the Bad Anthropocene is to be avoided.[188] Of course, the key difficulty is

---

[184] Spier, *Big History and the Future of Humanity*, 303.
[185] Spier, *Big History and the Future of Humanity*, 309–10.
[186] Spier, *Big History and the Future of Humanity*, 311.
[187] Christian, *Origin Story*, 282–3, 291–301. [188] Christian, *Origin Story*, 282.

preserving and continuing the 'good' developments that have occurred, without relying on the fossil fuel technologies that initially made them feasible. Christian recognizes that this is a central tension that makes it difficult to follow through with the goals set out in recent international climate change agreements. But he suggests that the Big History narrative includes several analogies that may guide the way forward. Chemical activation energies, for instance, only require an initial boost of energy to get going, at which point less energy is necessary. 'Perhaps we can think of fossil fuels as the activation energy that was needed to kickstart today's world', Christian suggests, and imagine new ways to keep the world 'going with smaller and more delicate energy flows'. Or perhaps the 'creative destruction' initially brought about by the adoption of fossil fuels could be considered 'the human equivalent of the gravitational energies that create stars. ... Like our sun, we can perhaps settle into a period of dynamic stability, having crossed a new threshold and built a new world society that preserves the best of the Good Anthropocene.'[189] This is where the analogical logic of Big History becomes entangled with wishful thinking.

This wishful thinking is tempered by the fact that, should these more stable cosmic processes somehow be replicable on a human scale, humans will likely have to accept a different way of living that places the ideal of sustainability ahead of growth, as Christian argues. But this will not happen unless governments are forced to adopt policies that will bring about this agenda, and this will in turn require 'the existence of voters who take the quest [for this new way of life] seriously. That will depend to some extent on how well and how persuasively people can describe the quest itself.'[190] Big History, therefore, is not just a cosmic story of humanity: it is also a description of the quest that the reader is expected to embrace in order to bring about a more equitable and sustainable world.

This quest of the future is further fleshed out in Christian's latest book, *Future Stories*, which seeks to ground the futuristic speculations of Big History within a rather vague theory of 'future thinking'. He argues that a form of future thinking was central to the evolution of all life, a form of thinking that became more prominent with the rise of collective learning that enabled a certain degree of directionality in subsequent human development, or what Christian calls 'future management'. The final part of the book speculates on how humans might manage the 'near' and 'middle' futures based on what the Big History narrative tells us about the past (there is also discussion of a 'remote' future, though this period is about the ultimate fate of the Earth and sun rather than humans per se). Whereas Christian postulates some rather fantastic scenarios

[189] Christian *Origin Story*, 294. [190] Christian, *Origin Story*, 300.

for the middle future, such as planetary migrations and the establishment of and reliance on nanotechnologies that will have virtually no environmental or energy costs, getting to these rather utopian futures depends on how 'we' manage the near future. That, for Christian, requires cooperation on a planetary scale. Unfortunately, Christian is forced to recognize that speculating on how such rhetorical cooperation might be put in practice is ultimately a fools' errand. That is because responding to the large-scale problems represented by the Anthropocene 'will depend on politics. And most political processes are too irregular to predict with confidence.'[191] This is no doubt true, and it begs an important question about the Big History project: if an understanding of human politics is so crucial to the managing of the near future, why are the political contingencies that shaped the past so decidedly absent from the Big History narrative?

The fact of the matter is that although Big History's futuristic conclusions are presented as following naturally from the stories of life that precede them, they actually represent a remarkable reversal of the logic of the Big History narrative. When such developments as the struggle for equal rights and democracy, the invention of medicine and birth control, and colonization and decolonization are presented as by-products of a particular regime of energy flows, it is difficult to imagine humans playing any intentional role in shaping the future course of history to some sort of desirable outcome. Yet this is the rhetorical compensation that the reader is offered at the end of a story that claims to uncover the true meaning of life as imparted by modern science, a well-worn strategy of evolutionary epics and other popular science publications.[192]

4 Conclusion

As this Element has shown, the attempt to unify historical knowledge under the framework of a grand conceptual apparatus has a long history. It may be true that all peoples have sought to situate their lives within creation myths or origin stories, but Big History's story is developed from one particular creation myth associated with the Christian sense of history. Big History is not a story of eternal recurrence nor is it derived from Dreaming; it is, rather, a linear narrative with a clear beginning and ending, punctuated by a series of stages that move the narrative forward, underpinned by a theory of historical change derived from physics. It is no doubt a remarkably successful example of what is often called 'teaching-led research', but this does not mean that it is somehow devoid of an

[191] Christian, *Future Stories*, 246.
[192] Schrempp, *The Ancient Mythology of Modern Science*, 208.

overarching philosophical perspective, a philosophical perspective that has a history.

Indeed, despite the fact that Big History is a story that stretches back to the origin of the cosmos and forward to eventual equilibrium, the diverse processes and events associated with cosmology, geology, biology, and human history are all situated on a single timeline in the same way that Ussher synchronized the events of the Bible with those of profane history or that Burnet made his sacred history of the Earth conform to the stages of universal history. Whereas the deep meaning of these narratives was derived from their reference to the transcendent, the writers of positivist universal histories and evolutionary epics of subsequent years claimed to uncover the deep meanings of history with reference not to God but rather to scientific paradigms. Timelines expanded, all of history was naturalized, and human development became a story of progress, no better instantiated than by the development of science itself. We should not be surprised, then, that Big History finds a key place on its own 13.8 billion year timeline as the eschaton of collective learning and the herald of humanity's salvation.

But as this Element has also shown, Big History's chief message of how its universalizing perspective will enable humans to overcome the large-scale problems of the present and near future is contradicted by its rootedness in a tradition of philosophical history that sees humans as the product of deterministic forces of nature. Moreover, its specialized discourse of complexity and thresholds and of Goldilocks circumstances and energy flows fails to explain the contingencies of human history. What we have instead is a hypothetical template of how history is imagined to occur from a cosmic perspective that claims to be scientific because relatively accurate dates can now be plotted on a singular timescale. But once the big historian drills down to examine particular human events, such as the development of birth control or the rise of democracy, the logic of Big History reduces these emergent realities to the status of predictable effects of an overarching drive for energy flows.[193]

This is not a problem that can be easily fixed, such as by engaging in more careful historical analysis, for it results from the grounding premises of Big History itself. Big historians are devoted to telling a single, universal story that presents itself as a unification of all historical knowledge, in line with E. O. Wilson's commitment to 'consilience'. Consequently, they are unable to deal with the fact that their scientific architecture may not be applicable to competing scales of time and action. Even if we accept that the nature of

[193] For a similar critique of the use of hypothetical scientific theories to explain complex or unknown historical events see Kleinberg, 'Just the Facts'.

anthropogenic climate change means that the different scales of time associated with the planet, geology, and human history have suddenly collided, this does not mean, as Chakrabarty puts it, 'that the related but different stories of humans as a divided humanity, as a species, and as a geological agent have all fused into one big geostory and that a single story of the planet and of history of life on it can now serve in the place of humanist histories'.[194] The history of the planet is simply not the same story as the history of humanity. These do need to be understood in relation to one another if humans are to be able to grapple with the reality of their present-day experiences of large-scale processes, such as those associated with climate change. But such a grappling requires a much more self-conscious reckoning with the complexities of human history in relation to other scales of time than Big History – with its devotion to universalism and consilience – is capable of providing.

---

[194] Chakrabarty, *The Climate of History in a Planetary Age*, 15.

Bibliography

Bain, Robert, 'Crossing Thresholds: Using Big History to Meet Challenges in Teaching and Learning in the United States', in Craig Benjamin, Esther Quaedackers, and David Baker (eds.), *The Routledge Companion of Big History*, pp. 372–94. London: Routledge, 2021.

Bashford, Alison, *The Huxleys: An Intimate History of Evolution*. Chicago: University of Chicago Press, 2022.

Benjamin, Craig, *The First Silk Roads Era: Empires and the Ancient World, 50 BCE–250 CE*. Cambridge: Cambridge University Press, 2018.

Benjamin, Craig, Esther Quaedackers, and David Baker (eds.), *The Routledge Companion to Big History*. London: Routledge, 2021.

Bossuet, Jacques-Bénigne, *Discourse on Universal History*, trans. Elborg Forster, ed. Orest Ranum. Chicago: University of Chicago Press, 1976.

Blanks, David, 'Science and Religion in Big History: The Dialogue Model', in Lowell Gustafson, Barry H. Rodrigue, and David Blanks (eds.), *Science, Religion, and Deep Time*, pp. 11-32. London: Routledge, 2022.

Brown, Cynthia Stokes, *Big History: From the Big Bang to the Present*. New York: New Press, 2007.

Buckle, Henry Thomas, *History of Civilization in England*, vol. 1. London: John W. Parker and Son, 1857.

Burchfield, Joe D., *Lord Kelvin and the Age of the Earth*. Chicago: University of Chicago Press, 1975.

Butler, Samuel, *Life and Habit*. London: Trübner, 1878.

Campbell, George (Duke of Argyll), *The Unity of Nature*. London: Alexander Strahan, 1884.

Carson, Rachel, *Silent Spring*. Boston: Houghton Mifflin, 1962.

Chaisson, Eric, 'Big History's Risk and Challenge', *Expositions* 8:1 (2014), 85–95.

Chaisson, Eric, *Cosmic Evolution: The Rise of Complexity in Nature*. Cambridge, MA: Harvard University Press, 1991.

Chakrabarty, Dipesh, *The Climate of History in a Planetary Age*. Chicago: University of Chicago Press, 2021.

[Chambers, Robert], *Vestiges of the Natural History of Creation*. London: John Churchill, 1844.

Christian, David, 'The Case for "Big History"', *Journal of World History* 2 (1991), 223–38.

Christian, David, *Future Stories: A User's Guide to the Future*. New York: Bantam Books, 2022.

Christian, David, *Living Water: Vodka and Russian Society on the Eve of Emancipation*. Oxford: Clarendon, 1990.

Christian, David, *Maps of Time: An Introduction to Big History*, 2nd ed. Berkeley: University of California Press, 2011.

Christian, David, *Origin Stories: A Big History of Everything*. London: Penguin Books, 2019.

Christian, David, 'The Return of Universal History', *History and Theory* 49 (December 2010), 6–27.

Christian, David, 'Silk Roads or Steppe Roads? The Silk Roads in World History', *Journal of World History* 11 (Spring 2000), 1–26.

Christian, David, 'A Single Historical Continuum', in David C. Krakauer, John Lewis Gaddis, and Kenneth Pomeranz (eds.), *History, Big History, and Metahistory*, pp. 11–37. Santa Fe: Santa Fe Institute, 2017.

Christian, David, 'What Is Big History?' *Journal of Big History* 1:1 (2018), 1–19.

Christian, David, Cynthia Stokes Brown, and Craig Benjamin, *Big History: Between Nothing and Everything*. New York: McGraw-Hill Education, 2014.

Comte, Auguste, *System of Positive Philosophy*, 4 vols., trans. J. H. Bridges et al. London: Longmans, Green, 1875–7.

Condorcet, Jean-Antoine-Nicolas de Caritat, marquis de, *Outlines of an Historical View of the Progress of the Human Mind*, English translation. London: J. Johnson, 1795.

Darwin, Charles, *The Autobiography of Charles Darwin, 1809–1882*, ed. Nora Barlow. London: Collins, 1958.

Dennett, Daniel C., *Darwin's Dangerous Idea: Evolution and the Meanings of Life*. London: Penguin, 1995.

Desmond, Adrian, *The Politics of Evolution: Morphology, Medicine, and Reform in Radical London*. Chicago: University of Chicago Press, 1989.

Diamond, Jared, *The Rise and Fall of the Third Chimpanzee: How Our Animal Heritage Affects the Way We Live*. New York: Vintage, 1991.

Drummond, Henry, *The Ascent of Man*. London: Hodder and Stoughton, 1894.

Edwards, Katherine, 'Why the Big History Project Funded by Bill Gates Is Alarming', *Guardian*, 10 September 2014, www.theguardian.com/commentisfree/2014/sep/10/big-history-bill-gates-uk-state-schools-education.

Feldherr, Andrew and Grant Hardy (eds.), *The Oxford History of Historical Writing*, vol. 1, *Beginnings to AD 600*. Oxford: Oxford University Press, 2011.

Frank, Andre Gunder, 'Universal History: Sizing up Humanity in Big History', *Journal of World History* 16:1 (2005), 83–97.

Galison, Peter and David J. Stump (eds.), *The Disunity of Science: Boundaries, Contexts, and Power*. Stanford: Stanford University Press, 1996.

Ghosh, Oroon K., 'Some Theories of Universal History', *Comparative Studies in Society and History* 7:1 (1964), 1–20.

Gould, Stephen Jay, 'Sociobiology: The Art of Storytelling', *New Scientist*, 16 November 1878, pp. 530–3.

Graeber, David and David Wengrow, *The Dawn of Everything: A New History of Humanity*. London: Allen Lane, 2021.

Grafton, Anthony, 'Joseph Scaliger and Historical Chronology: The Rise and Fall of a Discipline', *History and Theory* 14:2 (1975), 156–85.

Grafton, Anthony, 'Scaliger's Chronology: Early Patterns of Reception', in Nicholas Hardy and Dmitri Levitin (eds.), *Confessionalism and Erudition in Early Modern Europe: An Episode in the History of the Humanities*. Oxford: Oxford University Press, 2019, pp. 154–93.

Griggs, Tamara, 'Universal History from Counter-Reformation to Enlightenment', *Modern Intellectual History* 4:2 (2007), 219–47.

Gustafson, Lowell, Barry H. Rodrigue, and David Blanks (eds.), *Science, Religion, and Deep Time*. London: Routledge, 2022.

Harari, Yuval Noah, *Homo Deus: A Brief History of Tomorrow*. New York: Vintage, 2017.

Harari, Yuval Noah, *Sapiens: A Brief History of Human Kind*. New York: Vintage, 2015.

Harrison, Peter, 'Why Religion Is Not Going Away and Science Will Not Destroy It', *Aeon*, 7 September 2017, https://aeon.co/ideas/why-religion-is-not-going-away-and-science-will-not-destroy-it.

Hazard, Paul, *La Crise de la conscience européenne*. Paris: Boivin, 1935.

Hesketh, Ian, 'The First Darwinian: Alfred Russel Wallace and the Meaning of Darwinism', *Journal of Victorian Culture* 25 (April 2020), 174–84.

Hesketh, Ian, 'From Copernicus to Darwin to You: History and the Meaning(s) of Evolution', in Bernard Lightman (ed.), *Rethinking History, Science, and Religion: An Exploration of Conflict and the Complexity Principle*. Pittsburgh: University of Pittsburgh Press, 2019, pp. 191–205.

Hesketh, Ian, 'The Future Evolution of "Man"', in Efram Sera-Shriar (ed.), *Historicizing Humans: Deep Time, Evolution and Race in Nineteenth-Century British Sciences*. Pittsburgh: University of Pittsburgh Press, 2018, pp. 201–27.

Hesketh, Ian, 'A Good Darwinian? Winwood Reade and the Making of a Late Victorian Evolutionary Epic', *Studies in History and Philosophy of Biological and Biomedical Sciences* 51 (2015), 44–52.

Hesketh, Ian, 'The Recurrence of the Evolutionary Epic', *Journal of the Philosophy of History* 9:2 (2015), 196–219.

Hesketh, Ian, *The Science of History in Victorian Britain*. Pittsburgh: University of Pittsburgh Press, 2011.

Hesketh, Ian, 'The Story of Big History', *History of the Present* 4:2 (2014), 171–202.

Hesketh, Ian, 'What Big History Misses', *Aeon*, 16 December 2021, https://aeon.co/essays/we-should-be-wary-about-what-big-history-overlooks-in-its-myth.

Hesketh, Ian, 'Without a Darwinian Clue? Henry Thomas Buckle and the Naturalization of History', in Bernard Lightman and Efram Sera-Shriar (eds.), *Victorian Interdisciplinarity and the Sciences: Rethinking the Specialization Thesis*. Pittsburgh: University of Pittsburgh Press, 2024.

Hughes-Warrington, Marnie, with Anne Martin, *Big and Little Histories: Sizing Up Ethics in Historiography*. New York: Routledge, 2022.

Huxley, Julian, 'The Future of Man – Evolutionary Aspects', in Gordon Wolstenholme (ed.), *Man and His Future*. London: J. & A. Churchill, 1963, pp. 1–22.

Huxley, Julian, *Essays of a Humanist*. London: Chatto & Windus, 1964.

Huxley, Thomas Henry, 'On the Physical Basis of Life', in *Method and Results*, vol. 1. London: Macmillan, 1897, pp. 130–65.

Kant, Immanuel, 'Idea for a Universal History with Cosmopolitan Intent', trans. Carl J. Friedrich, in Allen W. Wood (ed.), *Basic Writings of Kant*. New York: The Modern Library, 2001, pp. 117–32.

Katerberg, William, 'Is Big History a Movement Culture?' *Journal of Big History* 2:1 (spring 2018), 63–72.

Kelly, Sean, *Becoming Gaia: On the Threshold of Planetary Initiation*. Olympia, WA: Integral Imprint, 2021.

Kleinberg, Ethan, 'Just the Facts: The Fantasy of a Historical Science', *History of the Present* 6:1 (2016), 87–103.

Lankester, E. R., *Degeneration: A Chapter in Darwinism*. London: Macmillan, 1880.

Lightman, Bernard, *Victorian Popularizers of Science: Designing Nature for New Audiences*. Chicago: University of Chicago Press, 2007.

Lightman, Bernard (ed.), *Global Spencerism: The Communication and Appropriation of a British Evolutionist*. Leiden: Brill, 2016.

Lineweaver, Charles H., 'Cosmic Perspectives and the Myths We Need to Survive', *Journal of Big History* 3:3 (2019), 81–93.

Livingstone, David N., *Adam's Ancestors: Race, Religion, and the Politics of Human Origins*. Baltimore: Johns Hopkins University Press, 2008.

Lloyd, G. E. R., 'Epilogue', in Andrew Feldherr and Grant Hardy (eds.), *The Oxford History of Historical Writing*, vol. 1, *Beginnings to AD 600*. Oxford: Oxford University Press, 2011, pp. 601–20.

Löwith, Karl, *Meaning in History*. Chicago: University of Chicago Press, 1949.

McNeill, J. R., *Something New Under the Sun: An Environmental History of the Twentieth-Century World*. New York: Norton, 2000.

Marincola, John, 'Universal History from Ephorus to Diodorus', in John Marincola (ed.), *A Companion to Greek and Roman Historiography*, vol. 1. Oxford: Blackwell, 2007, pp. 155–63.

Marsham, Andrew, 'Universal Histories in Christendom and the Islamic World *c.*700–*c.*1400', in Sarah Foot and Chase F. Robinson (eds.), *The Oxford History of Historical Writing*, vol. 2, *400–1400*. Oxford: Oxford University Press, 2012, pp. 431–56.

Meadows, Donella H., Dennis L. Meadows, Jørgen Randers, and William W. Behrens III, *The Limits to Growth*. New York: Universe Books, 1972.

Megill, Allan, '"Big History" Old and New: Presuppositions, Limits, Alternatives', *Journal of the Philosophy of History* 9 (2015), 306–26.

Megill, Allan, 'History's Unresolving Tensions: Reality and Implications', *Rethinking History* 23:3 (2019), 279–303.

Milam, Erika Lorraine, *Creatures of Cain: The Hunt for Human Nature in Cold War America*. Princeton: Princeton University Press, 2019.

Nienhauser, William H. 'Sima Qian and the *Shiji*', in Andrew Feldherr and Grant Hardy (eds.), *The Oxford History of Historical Writing*, vol. 1, *Beginnings to* AD *600*. Oxford: Oxford University Press, 2011, pp. 463–84.

Penman, Leigh T. I., *The Lost History of Cosmopolitanism: The Early Modern Origins of the Intellectual Ideal*. London: Bloomsbury, 2021.

Pick, Daniel, *Faces of Degeneration: A European Disorder, c.1818–1918*. Cambridge: Cambridge University Press, 1989.

Poole, William, *The World Makers: Scientists of the Restoration and the Search for the Origins of the Earth*. Oxford: Peter Lang, 2010.

Reade, Winwood, *Martyrdom of Man*. London: Trübner, 1872.

Reade, Winwood, *Martyrdom of Man*. London: Pemberton, 1968.

Rudwick, Martin J. S., *Earth's Deep History: How It Was Discovered and Why It Matters*. Chicago: University of Chicago Press, 2014.

Schilt, Cornelis J., *Isaac Newton and the Study of Chronology: Prophecy, History, and Method*. Amsterdam: Amsterdam University Press, 2021.

Schrempp, Gregory, *The Ancient Mythology of Modern Science: A Mythologist Looks (Seriously) at Popular Science Writing*. Montreal and Kingston: McGill-Queen's University Press, 2012.

Secord, James, *Victorian Sensation: The Extraordinary Publication, Reception, and Secret Authorship of* Vestiges of the Natural History of Creation. Chicago: University of Chicago Press, 2000.

Sideras, Lisa H., *Consecrating Science: Wonder, Knowledge, and the Natural World*. Berkeley: University of California Press, 2017.

Snobelen, David, 'William Whiston, Isaac Newton and the Crisis of Publicity', *Studies in History and Philosophy of Science* 35 (2004), 573–603.

Smail, Daniel Lord, *On Deep History and the Brain*. Berkeley: University of California Press, 2007.

Spier, Fred, *The Structure of Big History: From the Big Bang until Today*. Amsterdam: Amsterdam University Press, 1996.

Spier, Fred, *Big History and the Future of Humanity*, 2nd ed. Chichester: Wiley Blackwell, 2015.

Sorkin, Andrew Ross, 'So Bill Gates Has This Idea for a History Class . . .', *The New York Times*, 5 September 2014, www.nytimes.com/2014/09/07/magazine/so-bill-gates-has-this-idea-for-a-history-class.html.

Sullivan, Tracy, 'The *Big History Project* in Australia', in Lowell Gustafson, Barry H. Rodrigue, and David Blanks (eds.), *Science, Religion, and Deep Time*. London: Routledge, 2022, pp. 339–60.

Swimme, Brian, and Thomas Berry, *The Universe Story: The Primordial Flaring Forth to the Ecozoic Era – A Celebration of the Unfolding of the Cosmos*. New York: HarperCollins, 1992.

Thomas, Julia Adeney, Mark Williams, and Jan Zalasiewicz, *The Anthropocene: A Multidisciplinary Approach*. Cambridge: Polity Books, 2020.

Topham, Jonathan R., *Reading the Book of Nature: How Eight Best Sellers Reconnected Christianity and the Sciences on the Eve of the Victorian Age*. Chicago: University of Chicago Press, 2022.

Volk, Tyler, 'The Metapattern of General Evolutionary Dynamics and the Three Dynamical Realms of Big History', *Journal of Big History* 4:3 (2020), 31–53.

Weidman, Nadine, *Killer Instinct: The Popular Science of Human Nature in Twentieth-Century America*.Cambridge, MA: Harvard University Press, 2021.

Wells, H. G., *The Outline of History: Being a Plain History of Life and Mankind*, 2 vols. New York: Macmillan, 1920.

Wells, H. G., Julian Huxley, and G. P. Wells, *Evolution: Fact and Theory*. London: Cassell, 1934.

Wilson, Edward O., *On Human Nature*. Cambridge, MA: Harvard University Press, 1978.

Wilson, Edward O., *Consilience: The Unity of Knowledge*. New York: Vintage, 1998.

Woolf, Daniel, *A Global History of History*. Cambridge: Cambridge University Press, 2011.

Woolf, Daniel, 'Historical Periodization: A Defence', unpublished MS, quoted with permission of the author.

Wright, T. R., *The Religion of Humanity: The Impact of Comtean Positivism on Victorian Britain*. Cambridge: Cambridge University Press, 1986.

Yeo, Richard, 'Science and Intellectual Authority in Mid-Nineteenth-Century Britain', *Victorian Studies* 28:1 (1984), 5–31.

Cambridge Elements

Historical Theory and Practice

Daniel Woolf

Queen's University, Ontario

Daniel Woolf is Professor of History at Queen's University, where he served for ten years as Principal and Vice-Chancellor, and has held academic appointments at a number of Canadian universities. He is the author or editor of several books and articles on the history of historical thought and writing, and on early modern British intellectual history, including most recently *A Concise History of History* (Cambridge University Press 2019). He is a Fellow of the Royal Historical Society, the Royal Society of Canada, and the Society of Antiquaries of London. He is married with three adult children.

Editorial Board

About the Series

Cambridge Elements in Historical Theory and Practice is a series intended for a wide range of students, scholars, and others whose interests involve engagement with the past. Topics include the theoretical, ethical, and philosophical issues involved in doing history, the interconnections between history and other disciplines and questions of method, and the application of historical knowledge to contemporary global and social issues such as climate change, reconciliation and justice, heritage, and identity politics.

Cambridge Elements

Historical Theory and Practice

Elements in the Series

The Theory and Philosophy of History: Global Variations
João Ohara

A History of Political Science
Mark Bevir

The Transformation of History in the Digital Age
Ian Milligan

Historians' Virtues: From Antiquity to the Twenty-First Century
Herman Paul

Confronting Evil in History
Daniel Little

Progress and the Scale of History
Tyson Retz

Collaborative Historical Research in the Age of Big Data: Lessons from an Interdisciplinary Project
Ruth Ahnert, Emma Griffin, Mia Ridge and Giorgia Tolfo

A History of Big History
Ian Hesketh

A full series listing is available at: www.cambridge.org/EHTP

Printed in the United States
by Baker & Taylor Publisher Services